THE
BACKPACKER'S COMPANION

THE
BACKPACKER'S COMPANION

AN INSIDER'S LOOK AT THE EQUIPMENT, TECHNIQUES, TRAILS, AND VISTAS

Sharon AvRutick and Joseph Wallace

Principal Photography by
Tom Stack & Associates

SMITHMARK

A FRIEDMAN GROUP BOOK
This edition published in 1992
by SMITHMARK Publishers Inc.
112 Madison Avenue
New York, New York 10016

ISBN 0-8317-6693-X

THE BACKPACKER'S COMPANION
was prepared and produced by
Michael Friedman Publishing Group, Inc.
15 West 26th Street
New York, NY 10010

Editor: Suzanne DeRouen
Art Director: Jeff Batzli
Designer: Lynne Yeamans
Illustrator: Martin Schneebalg
Photography Editor: Christopher C. Bain

Front jacket photography, clockwise from top:
© Sharon Gerig/Tom Stack & Associates,
© Keith Murakami/Tom Stack & Associates,
© Bob Winsett/Tom Stack & Associates,
© W. Banaszewski/Visuals Unlimited

Back jacket photography: © Christopher C. Bain

Additional photocredits: p. 114, © Lynn Gerig/Tom Stack & Associates; p. 128, © Christopher C. Bain;
p. 142, © Anne E. Zuckerman/Tom Stack & Associates; p. 152, © Manfred Gottschalk/Tom Stack & Associates; p. 168, © Sharon Gerig/Tom Stack & Associates.

Typeset by Bookworks Plus
Color separation by United South Sea Graphic Art Co., Ltd.
Printed and bound in Hong Kong by Leefung-Asco Printers, Ltd.

DEDICATION

To our next joint project.

TABLE OF CONTENTS

INTRODUCTION

"So you're writing *The Backpacker's Companion.* Just what the world needs—another guide to what expensive gear to buy!" Such sarcasm dogged us more than once when we began to describe this book. So let's get it straight right from the start.

Unlike many books for backpackers, this one will not read like a catalogue of name brands. We are not interested in pushing one manufacturer's goods or dissecting another's failings. We don't name names. Though we will talk at length about what types of gear you can find in the store, please keep in mind that you should not run out and yank it off the shelf. We're not trying to get you to buy, buy, buy.

Instead, we'll attempt to give you the information you need so that you'll be able to make your own decisions. We won't tell you what brand of pack is best; we'll tell you how to decide for yourself. We won't encourage you to splurge on a new pair of lightweight synthetic boots if you're happy with your old leather ones. We won't tell you what trails to hike; we'll describe a whole lot of them that many backpackers have enjoyed. We won't legislate how far you should hike and how much you should carry; we'll tell you how to figure it out for yourself.

The fact is, there's no one "right" tent or "perfect" trail. There are a lot of them—and the one you pick depends on who you are and what you're looking for. You've got to decide for yourself.

That's one of the things we like about backpacking. It's what you make it. With a modicum of knowledge, preparation, and experience—and a generous helping of common sense—anyone can do it.

There's no getting around it: There are many things to look for on the trail, and a designer label isn't one of them. There are probably as many reasons why people hike as there are hikers.

A trail offers untold possibilities; you never know exactly what is around the next bend. There is no sense of predictability.

A trail gives you the opportunity to stretch yourself physically, to meet a challenge and rise to it.

A trail is a road away from "civilized" life; if you give yourself the chance, you'll see glorious views, plants, animals, the sky, the stars. There are no deadlines, no fuel bills, no blasting radios.

Opposite page: Paria Canyon, Utah.

The Snowmass Wilderness area in Colorado promises these backpackers a challenging and satisfying trail.

A trail is also a path into yourself; hiking, you have time to think, to wonder, to pause. There are no ringing phones, no distractions.

When people ask us why we hike ("You could take the car!") and wonder why we like to go camping ("I had enough of that when I was in the Girl Scouts!"), we don't always know how to respond. Sure, it can be uncomfortable. And, sure, sometimes it's just plain hard work.

But, to us and to millions of other hikers around the world, it's more than worth the effort. We hope this book will make the reasons abundantly clear.

Navajo Basin, San Miguel Mountains, Colorado.

C H A P T E R O N E

Chiricahua National Monument, Arizona.

GET READY, GET SET

A few years ago, we were camping in a relatively deserted campground in the Chiricahua mountains of southeastern Arizona. It had been a long day—hours on the plane to Tucson and then miles on the road to this relatively remote (and breathtakingly gorgeous) area. After a too-short hike to take a look around, we realized that dusk was falling in the mountain valley, so we pitched our tent in an inviting, sandy spot under some trees about one hundred feet from a river. We made a fire and ate a hasty meal. We were tired—overtired, really—excited, and on edge from a day filled with drastic change from big city to big country. We were suffering from an overabundance of adrenaline, not to mention an acute case of culture shock.

The security of a tent after dark will help you rest more peacefully.

After a while, we climbed into our sleeping bags and actually managed to fall into a restless sleep.

Then, suddenly—it seemed like mere moments later—we were both wide awake, hearts pounding. There was something outside the tent. Something big. Something close. A huge shape just an arm's length away was silhouetted against the bright light of the moon.

Suddenly, loudly, violently, it snorted. A low rasping animal sound. The sound a monster makes.

And it was answered by another off to the right. And then—*oh my god!* — another, and another, and another.

We were surrounded.

Now, anyone not suffering from first-night-out jitters would have put a few things together: No, it can't be bears—bears don't travel in herds. No, it can't be peccaries—the things outside are too big. No, it can't be the bogey monster....

But not us. We lay there, eyes bugging out, hearts pounding, frozen in fear.

Eventually, though, silence fell, and a quick look around with the flashlight showed us that we were again alone. After a while, we were even able to get back to sleep.

When the sun rose, we got up to examine the tracks the monsters had left in the sandy soil. You didn't have to be an Indian scout to recognize them: deer. Black-tailed deer.

JITTERS

It's taken years for us to be able to tell this story without blushing. It *is* embarrassing, but the fact is, we're not the only ones ever to feel this way. The first few nights out can be tough.

In fact, nighttime worries about lions, tigers, and bogey monsters are probably what keep many people forever off the trails and away from the campsites.

But even experienced backpackers are well acquainted with the fear that accompanies nights in the wilderness; they learn to expect it. And all of them have developed their own ways of dealing with it.

If you're well prepared, you're more likely to sleep. Talk to rangers and other hikers—find out what's around you. If there are a lot of other campers around, you can expect more noise in the night. If you're alone in the backcountry, learn what type of animal might pass through. And store your food in a way that doesn't encourage night visitors. There's nothing more frightening than not knowing what's out there finishing off your next meal.

Some backpackers like to camp next to a waterfall or rushing stream, because they provide white noise and make it easier to sleep.

Others swear by the relaxing powers of herbal tea, warm milk, Ovaltine, or brandy just before bedtime.

Still others insist that the best way to be sure you'll sleep at night is to hike vigorously during the day: Fatigue leads to sleep.

Sure, these things will help. But remember that culture shock isn't easy to banish. The fact is, no matter what you do, you may still be nervous.

There will be other mental challenges on your trip. To be best prepared, spend some time thinking your way through what lies ahead before you leave. That way, when you're actually on the trail, it'll be easier to fall right into the spirit of your adventure and get the most out of it.

THE FIRST STEP: WALKING

Don't forget the physical demands. No matter how well prepared you are mentally, if your body isn't up to the challenge, you're not going to have a good time.

Walking itself is so simple, even a child can do it. But how long does it take children to really master the feat of staying on their feet? And how many of us are so good at it that once we become adults we never trip and fall over?

Watch your step when attempting to cross rocky streams or rivers.

© John D. Cunningham/Visuals Unlimited

TRY LIFTING YOUR KNEES EXTRA HIGH WHEN GOING UPHILL. YOU'LL BE SURPRISED AT HOW MUCH EASIER IT IS TO MAKE PROGRESS USING THIS EFFICIENT MARCHING STRIDE THAN IT IS DRAGGING YOUR FEET.

The amazing thing about walking, really, is that we can do it at all. To make the heap of bones and tissue that we call the human body stand erect is hard enough, and then, on top of that, we want it to move. We ask our 650 muscles to move our 206 bones in defiance not only of the law of gravity, but of various other Newton's Laws as well.

It's actually such a complex procedure that scientists, from Leonardo da Vinci to today's high-tech researchers, still aren't entirely sure how it works.

THE SPORT OF WALKING

Despite its complexity, most of us do actually manage to master it. And, although hiking may never become an Olympic event, that doesn't make it any less of a sport. Neither does it make a hiker less than an athlete.

Carrying a sixty-pound pack up and down mountains fifteen miles a day is not a task to be taken lightly. But, then, for those unaccustomed to physical activity, neither is a more leisurely day spent walking in a local nature preserve.

In the same way that you can—if you are in reasonably decent condition—pick up and go skiing, swimming, jogging, or horseback riding without training for it, you can, of course, also go hiking.

But if you want to take an extended hike or carry a heavy pack, get in shape first. You won't risk a trip-spoiling injury. You'll enjoy your hike more while you're out there doing it, and you'll suffer from it less once you get back. (Have you ever gone back to the office after a backpacking adventure and thrilled your co-workers with tales of your derring-do—but been unable to climb down the stairs?)

Just as you would before starting any sort of new physical activity, check with your physician first. Then get in shape.

GETTING IN SHAPE

The main thing to do is: do something.

If you somehow missed the fitness boom of the '80's, you may not know that there are many books and magazine articles available these days that will explain the benefits of aerobic exercise to you in great detail. They'll help you set up an exercise program that's right for you, and explain why it works. Do some research. And then do some exercise.

Depending on your level of fitness, ability, and taste, try jogging, swimming, aerobics, dance, or biking. All, done regularly, will help strengthen your heart and lungs and get you in shape. You don't have to stick with just one activity—cross-training will help prevent boredom and injury. No matter what you do, stick with it on a regular basis.

Purists say the best way to get in shape for walking is to walk, walk, walk. And then walk some more.

And they're not necessarily wrong. Walking is such a gentle, natural movement that it's really not too hard to get going. It's easier to integrate into your day than any other form of activity.

Set realistic goals. If you've been a couch potato for years, you might want to begin with several laps around the block a few mornings a week. Late afternoons, when it's cool out, are also a good time to walk.

Ask yourself if you really need to drive to the store, to the station, to the office. Then walk instead.

Don't worry about your speed. Just try to increase the amount of time you spend on your feet. Where you're going doesn't matter; that you're taking the time to get there does.

Invite a friend to join you. For some people, conversation or just plain companionship helps the minutes and the miles (and the pounds) melt away. If no one you know is interested, think about joining a local hiking club.

Or go on your own. Bring a small personal stereo, or just savor the silence and the solitude.

On weekends, explore the trails in a local park or nature preserve. Carry a daypack with a water bottle, some snacks, and a nature guide. Get used to carrying the weight. Try long loops some days, shorter ones other days. Get used to climbing hills.

Keep exercising. While you stick with your aerobic exercise, start doing some of the specialized routines below that will help build your back and leg muscles, the muscles you'll use the most.

Remember, for maximum effect, perform each of these exercises slowly, smoothly, and deliberately.

Repetition is what it's all about. Start with a number that is reasonable for you. Do it every day. As the exercise gets easier—every week or so, perhaps—add a few repetitions.

Pay attention to your body. Pain is not necessarily gain, though some soreness is inevitable with any new exercise regimen.

Stretch before you start and after you finish.

The best way to get in shape for hiking is to walk.

High-altitude jogging is a great way to prepare for long, strenuous hikes.

SIT-UPS

You know how to do sit-ups. Just remember to keep your knees bent and your feet flat on the floor. Tuck your toes under a piece of furniture. Keep your hands behind your head, and move deliberately.

Sit-ups will strengthen your abdominal and lower back muscles, making it much easier for you to carry a heavy pack.

PUSH-UPS

You're also familiar with push-ups. We've all seen them done, but relatively few of us (especially women) can actually do them.

So consider beginning with "negative" push-ups, starting in the upper position (arms straightened) and lowering slowly down to the traditional starting point.

Or do "half" push-ups, with your knees on the floor, just raising and lowering your torso.

Just keep it up, and eventually you'll not only be doing "regular" push-ups, but shouldering a heavy pack with ease.

SHOULDER SHRUG

Though packs are designed so that you'll carry much of their weight with the big muscles of your hips and lower torso, your shoulders will have to, ahem, shoulder their share as well.

To get them in shape, hold five- or ten-pound weights, bricks, or a bag of books or cans in each hand. Stand up straight, arms down by your side, and slowly raise your shoulders and let them back down.

KNEE AND ANKLE LIFTS

It's easy to twist a knee or ankle while hiking, so strengthen the muscles around those vulnerable joints to protect them. If you are prone to knee strains, always wear some form of support, such as a brace, while you are on the trail.

To work on your knees, attach weights, a heavy can, or a small bag of sand to your ankles and sit on the edge of a table or counter. Your feet should not touch the floor. Slowly raise, straighten, and lower one leg at a time.

Then move the weight down to your toes, and raise and lower your feet in much the same way to build up your ankles.

ATTENTION

TRY THIS TRAIL **ONLY** IF YOU ARE IN TOP PHYSICAL CONDITION, WELL CLOTHED AND CARRYING EXTRA CLOTHING AND FOOD. MANY HAVE DIED ABOVE TIMBERLINE FROM EXPOSURE. TURN BACK AT THE FIRST SIGN OF BAD WEATHER.

WHITE MOUNTAIN NATIONAL FOREST

IN THE GYM

If you go to a gym or health club, take advantage of the weights and exercise machines there. Get a trainer to help you design a program for your needs.

In *The Outdoor Athlete* (Cordillera Press), author and fitness trainer Steve Ilg describes various training programs he recommends. Some specific exercises include:

Leg presses (you push a weight away from you with your legs on a leg-press machine) help condition thigh muscles.

Pull-ups (those same pull-ups you were supposed to do in high school) are great for your shoulders and arms.

Ilg claims back squats (basically, deep knee bends with a free weight resting on your shoulders behind your neck) are one of the best exercises a backpacker can do.

Remember, before doing any of these exercises make sure you are doing them right.

OTHER IDEAS

Walk or jog up and down hills or stairs, over and over again. When you're ready, put on your daypack (with a light load in it) and do it some more. If you're planning to carry a heavy pack in a hilly or mountainous area, try to practice this exercise with your fully loaded pack. Ignore the comments of your family and neighbors.

If you possibly can, take a few practice hikes with a fully loaded pack in the weeks before you go. The more you walk with a heavy pack, the easier it gets as your body adjusts itself to the extra load.

REALITY CHECK

Don't lose perspective.

What are your goals? If you simply want to get fit enough to enjoy a dayhike or two, you don't have to train like you're planning to through-hike the Appalachian Trail. What are your capabilities? If you're already in good shape, try just focusing on the muscles you need to strengthen.

Hiking is supposed to be fun, after all.

Now you're almost ready to go backpacking. You've worked hard to get in shape, and you're eager to be off.

But first you've got to ask yourself some questions.

Stretching and keeping your flexibility are vital in avoiding stiff, painful muscles after a day on the trail.

ALWAYS LEAVE A NOTE WITH A RELIABLE PERSON SAYING WHERE YOU'RE PLANNING TO GO AND WHEN YOU'RE PLANNING TO RETURN. BE AS SPECIFIC AS YOU CAN BE, ALLOWING FOR SOME ON-THE-TRAIL DECISION-MAKING LATITUDE. THIS IS ESPECIALLY IMPORTANT IF YOU'RE GOING OUT ALONE OR IN DANGEROUS CONDITIONS.

Where?

So where are you going? If you don't have a specific place in mind, talk to people who know the area you're interested in, and listen to their suggestions. Rangers are good sources of information for local, state, and national parks. The folks who work in outdoor stores or who run or belong to hiking clubs can also be founts of wisdom on the subject. *Backpacker* and *Outside* magazines offer plentiful tips, as do shelves full of books in stores specializing in outdoor gear. (Also check Chapters 9 and 10 in this book!)

Why?

What are your goals for this trip? To go further than man has gone before? Or to savor a few miles of hiking with a few solid periods of hanging out scattered liberally throughout? Your plans should reflect this.

When?

How much time do you have? You'll have to plan your equipment needs, your food supplies, and your itinerary accordingly. Try to be conservative.

What time of year will you be going? What's the weather going to be like? Check to find out the average temperature and precipitation in the area you're going to, but don't forget to check the five-day forecast for something a little more useful just before you hit the trails.

Staying found in Colorado's Lost Creek Wilderness.

© Spencer Swanger/Tom Stack & Associates

Trekking together in Nepal.

Who?

Unless you're going alone (which presents its own set of problems and questions, discussed in-depth in Chapter 8), your first major challenge will be to find the right partner. While a good friend or a spouse is the perfect dinner companion, frictions may develop once you are out on the trail, away from all other human companionship, living under conditions of relative discomfort. You may have different goals and different capacities.

If you're planning a dayhike or an overnight, you obviously don't need to worry too much about this. No matter the conflict, you should be able to survive that long, maybe even with your relationship intact.

But if you're heading out for a longer period of time, make sure you've found a kindred spirit. Get to know your partner on the trail. Take a couple of weeklong practice hikes together. If you can handle that comfortably, you should be able to handle a longer trek.

How?

Whatever you have in mind, plan it. Make sure you get at least one good map (experienced backcountry backpackers recommend taking at least two) of the area to tell you what to expect. Is the route you have in mind very hilly or very flat? Are there alternate trails in case the one you've picked doesn't please you? Where are the water resources?

Are you going into the backcountry? If you're planning a backcountry hike in a national park or a national forest, you will more than likely need a permit. The number of backcountry permits in popular areas is limited, so you'll have to plan ahead.

Before you hit the trails, it's a very good idea to take a first-aid or mountain-medicine course. You should also know how to use a map and compass, how to tie some simple knots, how to use and repair all your gear on your own, and how to build that most-important campfire.

Take the time to gather the skills you'll need. Don't depend on your companions to do all the work or to teach you along the way. Not only is that attitude counter to the spirit of teamwork necessary to make even a short trip a success, but it can be downright dangerous, as well. What if you get separated from the one person who really knows how to use a compass? What if your fire-building friend is off doing something else and you want to build a fire? What if you get lost and need to fend for yourself for a day or two? What if you have to ford a rushing stream with a heavy pack?

What If?

There are so many "what ifs" involved in any outdoor adventure. To somehow reconcile the unknown with your abilities is the key to confidence. Mastery of outdoor skills can mean the difference between a wonderful time and a miserable one—but they can also save your life.

With good planning, the necessary skills, decent physical conditioning, a clear understanding of your own limitations, good equipment, plenty of food and water, and a sense of humor, your backpacking trip will be a success.

C H A P T E R T W O

© Bob Winsett/Tom Stack & Associates

WHAT TO BRING: CLOTHING

In the past few years, outdoor clothing has come out of the closet. While stylish versions of hiking clothes are turning up in the windows of fashionable boutiques, hiking clothes themselves are developing some style. (Some are also developing style in lieu of quality, however, so beware.)

No matter how chic and outdoorsy we may seem, what we really need is comfort and protection from the elements. Recent years have brought new synthetic "miracle" fabrics to the market—fabrics that many people feel have some properties that make them superior to the traditional wool, cotton, and leather. They can provide better insulation, waterproofing, and durability, and they weigh less, to boot.

Keeping dry: the key to a good time.

IF YOUR BOOTS GET WET, DRY THEM SLOWLY AND CAREFULLY—NEVER IN DIRECT HEAT. REMEMBER TO CLEAN AND WATERPROOF LEATHER BOOTS REGULARLY. USE A PREPARATION THAT'S MADE FOR THE TYPE OF LEATHER YOUR BOOT IS MADE OF.

© Stewart M. Green/Tom Stack & Associates

Some people have jumped on the synthetic bandwagon, throwing out their old clothes and hitting the trails in nothing that doesn't have a trademark symbol after its name. Others still swear by the tried-and-true; what was good enough for them a few years ago still works today. Most of us have one foot in both worlds—we top our favorite wool sweater with a high-tech synthetic shell, wear wool pants with polypropylene long underwear, put our silk liners inside acrylic pile mittens.

One thing everyone agrees on, however, is that no matter what clothes you wear, you've got to layer. Layering traps the heat your body produces and holds it there, close to your skin. The more layers you wear, the more heat is trapped. The fewer layers you wear, the cooler you'll be.

Layering also protects the body by keeping it dry. A carefully chosen first layer will quickly remove perspiration from the skin while staying dry itself.

Layering is an obvious, simple solution to the problem of adaptation to variations in temperature and exertion. If it's chilly out, don't rely on one heavy garment to do all the work itself. Layer. All the layers may seem excessive at first, but by the middle of the hike, you will be grateful.

What do you really need? It all depends on what time of year it is, what the weather is, where you're going, and what you're going to be doing when you get there—not to mention your metabolism. Some backpackers take only enough clothing for one day—one full day. They'll start the day off wearing all the clothes they have, and then they will shed them as they move along and the day gets warmer. As evening approaches, every piece of clothing gets put back on, layer by layer.

Others, especially beginners, can't resist taking a few extra things "just in case." For them, experience is the best teacher: Beginners quickly learn to pare down, to take only what they'll really use.

Ask a group of backpackers what they feel is an absolute "must" on a camping trip, and you're asking for chaos. But this notoriously disagreeing crowd actually can agree on two things that you really should have: good boots and good rain gear.

RAIN GEAR:
A HARD RAIN'S GONNA FALL

No matter what the weather forecast says, no matter the season, no matter the climate: The only thing that will absolutely, positively guarantee that no rain falls on you during your trip is to bring your rain gear.

Rain gear is one of those backpacking must-haves for a very simple reason: It can not only make you more comfortable, but it can save your life. Cold wind can cool a wet body faster than you can say "hypothermia." (More on this in Chapter 6.)

In shopping for rain gear, there didn't used to be a huge choice. First, there was rubberized cotton. While a rainsuit made of this stuff might keep a fisherman dry in a downpour, a hiker wearing it would soon be drenched—not by rain, but by sweat. Rubberized materials simply don't breathe (those little metal-ringed "ventilation" holes simply don't ventilate sufficiently.) Also, they weigh a ton.

> DON'T WEAR COTTON UNDER A RAINSUIT. CHOOSE WOOL OR A SYNTHETIC AND YOU'LL STAY DRY AND COMFORTABLE.

TREAT THE SEAMS OF YOUR RAIN GEAR WITH SEAM SEALANT. BUT CHECK THE GARMENT'S LABELS FIRST.

Then there was coated nylon (or another synthetic fabric). Much lighter, these materials also take up less room in a pack. They even breathe a little. But most simply won't keep you dry. Often they're billed only as water-repellent (nice if it's not raining).

But now rain gear has entered the modern age. We have words like "microporous," and we have different proprietary waterproofing systems with high-tech names. We have Gore-Tex® and we have children of Gore-Tex®. All of these are very dependable and long lasting.

What this is all about is a simple fact of nature: In its gaseous state, water can pass through smaller openings than it can when liquid. Thus, vaporized sweat can escape through spaces rain can't penetrate. If you make a fabric with tiny little microscopic pores (hence "microporous") just the right size, you've got close to the ideal material for rain gear.

All the various companies in the rain gear business combine a microporous fabric with others (offering durability, extra insulation, and high-fashion colors) in various ways. Hence the proprietary waterproofing systems.

So which one works, you ask? If it were only that simple. If you simply swathed yourself in any of these fabrics, you'd probably stay dry. But could you walk? Could you carry a pack? Would you have any money left in the bank after you broke down and bought a rainsuit?

If you're broke, maybe you can get by with a poncho made of some standard (nonmicroporous) material. Ponchos are cheap, versatile (they'll also serve happily as a tarp or a lean-to in a pinch), and comfortable. But if it's windy, they tend to fly up, exposing you to the elements. The water will drain right off your head and shoulders, down your body, and then drip off—right onto your arms and legs. Cheap plastic ones rip. Ponchos can be great, though, in warm weather, particularly if you're going to be wearing shorts and you don't care if your legs get wet.

Some people swear by a cagoule, which is basically a long (knee-length), hooded anorak. Others are happy with just a rainjacket (again, they probably do most of their hiking in warm weather).

But if you're going to spend any substantial amount of time outdoors in the rain you're probably going to want a full rainsuit. So shop around. Talk to other hikers about their choices. See what's available in sizes that fit and colors you can tolerate. And think about how much you want to spend—high-tech water protection does not come cheap.

Even the cloudiest day in British Columbia can't hide the beauty of its lakes, snowcapped peaks, and jagged hillsides.

Also, look carefully for those all-too-common flaws that can make an otherwise-perfect rainsuit a leaky mess: Some zippers leak. Hoods fit some heads better than other heads. Some pants fall down easily, since they lack a belt. How do you feel about the noise yours makes when you walk? Are the pockets accessible and roomy? How quickly does the fabric dry? How much does the whole thing weigh? Is it reasonably well-made?

> IF YOUR HOOD DOESN'T DO THE JOB, TRY WEARING A BRIMMED WATERPROOF HAT UNDERNEATH IT.

Anything is possible if you're dressed right.

© Robert Winslow

BOOTS: ON YOUR FEET

We've all heard about the six thousand-mile trekkers who did it all in a worn-out pair of tennis shoes, and the retired military men who swear their old combat boots served them equally well in battle and on the trails. We recently saw a fellow hurrying up a mountain trail wearing a pack on his back and a pair of sandals on his feet. (He passed us, in fact.)

More power to them. Most of us, however, are happier in shoes designed to be walked in. And don't for a second think that the manufacturers don't know it. As if we didn't already have an abundance of choices, there they go, introducing new models, new designs, new styles every day of the week.

What's a hiker to do?

Stop. Think. Ask yourself what type of hiking you're going to be doing, and take a minute to learn about what goes into a good pair of boots.

Take it from the top: the *uppers*. The upper material must be flexible yet supportive, water-resistant or waterproof yet breathable, durable, strong, and attractive. The traditional boot has all-leather uppers, which offers the most

> DO YOU REALLY NEED TO WEAR BOOTS? IF YOU'RE NOT CARRYING A HEAVY PACK, AND IT'S NOT TOO ROCKY, YOU'LL PROBABLY BE OK IN STURDY RUNNING OR WALKING SHOES. THEY'RE LIGHTWEIGHT AND ARE EASIER ON THE TRAIL THAN HEAVY-SOLED BOOTS—ANOTHER PLUS.

A SHOELACE IS AN IMPORTANT PIECE OF EQUIPMENT. THERE ARE COTTON, RAWHIDE, AND NYLON SHOELACES. USE NYLON. THEY'LL LAST A LONG TIME AND DRY QUICKLY. THEY OFTEN ARE SLIPPERY, THOUGH, SO DOUBLE-KNOT THEM.

REMEMBER THAT BOOTS IN THE STORE WILL FIT DIFFERENTLY THAN BOOTS AT HOME. AND THOSE WILL FIT DIFFERENTLY FROM BOOTS ON THE TRAIL WHEN YOU'RE CARRYING A PACK. CHECK TO SEE IF YOUR STORE ACCEPTS RETURNS BEFORE YOU BUY.

durability and the best protection from the elements. But leather is heavy, and leather boots are expensive and require quite a break-in period. On the other hand, they'll last a long time. Newfangled boots use synthetic uppers (often nylon) reinforced with leather in key areas.

The *last* is the bootmaker's archetypical foot. Each bootmaker uses a different last, or a different type of last—none of which will likely match your foot. That's why it's important to try boots on.

Inside is, of course, the *lining*. This used to be exclusively leather, though today you'll find it's often been replaced by Cambrelle® (a soft, durable, synthetic) or another fabric. Whatever it's made of, a lining should breathe, absorb sweat, last a long time, offer some padding, and be just plain comfortable. Often, it's a matter of personal choice.

The *tongue* is another concern. Look for lots of padding and lots of comfort. It should fold up neatly under the laces, without creating any bumps or ridges that could cause blisters. It should also be big enough to keep water, snow, and rocks out.

There are various types of *lacing* systems—eyelets, speed lacing, and hooks. Most boots these days use a combination of the above, with one of the first two below and hooks on top.

Underneath, you've got your *sole*. Treads range from the heavy to moderate to practically nonexistent.

When you look at boots, try to determine how much support they offer (without being so stiff that you can't walk in them). You want to look for stiff heel counters, good arch support, and enough rigidity to prevent your feet from twisting.

OLD VS. NEW

So you go to a store. You're ready to buy some boots. You look up and are confronted with—can it be?—hundreds of choices. Boots in every color of the rainbow. Low boots, high boots. Cheap boots, expensive boots. American boots, foreign boots. Specialized boots, all-purpose boots.

Don't panic. It's all really very simple.

First, there are the traditional leather boots. Some backpackers will never give them up, arguing (not unreasonably) that they're unsurpassed for rough terrain, heavy load-carrying, warmth, and dryness. However, leather boots weigh quite a bit, and they'll take a good chunk out of your wallet.

Ask yourself if you'll really need them, and you may well find yourself joining large crowds of hikers in the move toward lighter-weight boots. These boots, which were introduced about a decade ago, combine the best of a couple of possible worlds. From the traditional leather boot, they borrow a serious lug sole and heavy-duty ankle support (for traction and stability). From the running shoe they make liberal use of nylon and other synthetics (for breathability, comfort, and light weight). They hardly need to be broken in at all, they're durable, and relatively inexpensive. They come in a wide variety of colors and fabrics (some waterproof). They're widely available.

Take your time examining the boots in the store, even before you try them on. You'll soon see that in many ways, some still resemble their running shoe ancestors more than others. Think about your own needs. Use your common sense. And don't be afraid to ask questions.

To fit a boot, first make sure you're wearing the same socks or combination of socks you'll actually take on the trails. Now lace them up: They should be loose in the toes, tight across the ankle, and looser again on top. Can you wiggle your toes? Good. Now take a walk. Convince the salesperson to let you wear them in the store for at least a good ten or fifteen minutes; this will allow time for your feet to adjust to the fit and even for some hot spots to develop if they're going to. Stand on your tiptoes. Your heels shouldn't slip. If the store has a slanted board to stand on, get up on it to make sure your toes won't hit the front of the boot when you're going downhill. Are you aware of any blister-causing seams?

Try on a few pairs to compare. Weight could be the deciding factor between two similar models. Someone once said a pound on the foot equals three on the back.

Check the price, of course—there can be a startlingly substantial difference between makes and models. Don't forget to shop around.

LONG UNDERWEAR: UNDERCOVER

Long johns, too, have evolved. Now presented with an almost mind-numbing selection from which to choose, we're far from the world of baggy flannels.

Before trying anything on, remember what long johns are supposed to do: The heart of the layering system, they have to keep you warm when you're cold, and keep you cool when you're not. If they get wet, they should dry

When buying boots, look for stiff heel counters, good arch support, and enough rigidity to prevent feet from twisting.

On the sign:

GIBBS BROOK SCENIC AREA

As you hike along the Crawford Path from here to the summit of Mt. Pierce, you will be passing through the Gibbs Brook Scenic Area. These 900 acres were set aside by the Forest Service to preserve its outstanding scenic and botanical qualities. This area contains one of the few extensive stands of virgin red spruce and balsam fir existing in the northeast.

WHITE MOUNTAIN National Forest

Trekking along snow-filled Crawford Path in the White Mountains.

quickly, without sapping heat from the body. They should wick perspiration away from the skin. They should fit tightly but comfortably, not itch, and also be presentable enough to serve as outerwear if necessary.

So what miracle fibers are capable of so much? You can be sure most came out of a test tube. As with so much outdoor gear these days, synthetic materials seem to be in the forefront. But there's still wool and silk, holding their own, though they're not so good once they get wet.

Polypropylene, now an old-timer in the long john world, can combine all the wonders that new technology has wrought with a soft feel and a comfortable fit. Old polypro had a well-earned reputation for its less-than-sweet perfume; after only a very few wearings, it tended to take on a stink that would never quite wash out. The newfangled type is better, but consider yourself forewarned. Other synthetics include myriad combinations of polyester, lycra, and nylon.

It's hard to believe that fishnet underwear works—it's full of holes!—but many swear by it. The point is, of course, that while it doesn't work on its own, when teamed with another layer, it traps warm air against the skin. One negative is the imprint it leaves on your skin.

Some manufacturers offer a variety of choices depending on exertion level and temperature. Check the package for details. Remember that if you're going to be active, it's better to go light with the long johns, and cover them up with warmer layers.

In terms of styling and fit, you've just got to try them on. Some fit; some don't. You'll like some; you'll hate others. You may do well with bottoms of one style, fabric, or manufacturer and tops of another.

Bottoms, by the way, are pretty much all styled the same (though some men's models have an exposed fly and some don't), but the variety in tops is worth noting: You can get a regular turtleneck, a zippered turtleneck, a crew neck, or even a tank top. Some people recommend the zippered T-neck for its flexibility. Just make sure the zipper doesn't irritate your throat or neck.

PANTS: THE LOWER HALF

Wear what's comfortable. If it's hot and you're on a clear trail, wear shorts. If there are a lot of brambles or poison ivy, ticks, winds, strong sun, high altitude, or any one of a number of other things, though, wear long pants. (Many people never wear shorts.) Pants come in so many different materials these days that you should certainly be able to find something that's comfortable and practical for your uses.

Blue jeans are not recommended for hiking: Not only do they restrict free movement, but they also provide little in the way of insulation, and once they get wet, they stay wet. There are true stories of jeans-wearing hikers lost in severe northern storms who died before they could be rescued; their wet jeans sucked the heat right out of their bodies.

Many backpackers find that shorts and long johns are the leg coverings of their choice.

We've all seen pictures of cheerful European hikers scampering down trails in their knickers. Somehow, these practical alternatives haven't caught on widely in the United States. Some individuals do swear by them, though, proclaiming knickers, being neither shorts nor long pants, offer the best of both worlds.

> BE KIND TO YOUR FEET. TAKE A BREAK NEAR A STREAM EVERY NOW AND THEN AND LET THEM LUXURIATE IN THE COOL, FRESH WATER. AT THE END OF THE DAY, MASSAGE THEM. RUB, PULL, PRESS, POKE—THEY'LL THANK YOU FOR IT.

One leg at a time in British Columbia.

© Spencer Swanger/Tom Stack & Associates

Layers will set you free.

TOPS: SHIRT UP

Wear whatever you want. Deciding what type of shirt to wear when you're backpacking isn't really very different from doing it at home.

If it's hot, wear a T-shirt, though you might want to consider a long-sleeved cotton shirt to protect you from the sun. (Some people avoid tank tops, because without a protecting layer between them, their pack straps irritate their shoulders.)

If it's cool, put a wool, flannel, or chamois shirt over the first shirt, and be sure that the first shirt is made of some material that will wick your perspiration away.

SWEATERS, JACKETS, VESTS: BUNDLE UP

This layer is also self-explanatory. Just make sure that whatever you choose is comfortable, nonbinding, and easy to get on and off.

For that reason, very bulky sweaters are probably better left at home. Consider instead a couple of lighter sweaters or a pile jacket. Pile is soft, lightweight, and as warm as wool, even when wet. Rolled up, a pile garment serves another useful purpose; it makes a fabulous pillow. It's not windproof or waterproof, however, which you must take into consideration before you take to the trail.

Incredibly lightweight and warm, down-filled or quilted vests are also effective layers. Look for one with snaps or high-quality zippers and insulated pockets.

SHELLS AND JACKETS: COVER UP

This ultimate layer is your main ally in the ongoing battle against the unpredictable elements. All those internal layers work hard to keep your body warm and dry from the inside out, while the outer layer works to do the same thing from the outside in.

With so many choices available, you won't have a problem finding something to do the job effectively. But you do have to decide what job you need done. A lightweight nylon anorak shell will do the trick in many situations, but a heavier insulated garment may be called for if you're going to be in particularly frigid conditions.

A hood can come in handy, so make sure it fits; a small hood is almost as bad as no hood at all. Also make sure it has a drawstring to keep it on. Will it fit over a hat?

If your garment has a zipper, make sure it's as high quality as the garment itself. No matter how warm the jacket is, it's not going to do you much good if the zipper breaks. Nylon is better than metal. Zippers that open from the top and bottom are remarkable conveniences and are easier to manipulate in cold weather conditions.

Admiring the view of the Park Range, Colorado.

HATS: USE YOUR HEAD

It's true, you really should wear a hat to protect yourself from the cold, just like your mother always said.

In the winter, it'll keep you warm (the head is a notorious culprit in the fight to avoid heat loss). You'll find that you can dress more lightly or wear fewer layers if you've got your hat on. Wool, wool-felt, synthetic knits, and pile will all do the job. Look for a model with a chin strap, a visor, and earflaps. A face mask may be necessary in extreme cold.

In warm weather, a hat (a different, lighter hat, obviously) will actually keep you cooler by keeping the sun off the top of your head and face. Look for a fishing cap or a baseball or cycling cap made of cotton or cotton blends. Light colors will deflect some of the sun's heat. Hats are especially important in the summer to fend off sunburn and heatstroke.

SOCKS: FOR HAPPY FEET

Take care of your feet. Keep them happy and they'll take care of you.

Many people wear two pairs of socks when hiking; some even wear three for extra warmth and absorption. There's a new generation of special sport-specific socks on the market now which include, among others, socks for running, hiking, tennis, and walking. They have extra padding and support where you need it and are soft to the touch. Some people love this fancy footware, but others feel they aren't worth the price.

If you're going to wear two pairs, your liners or inner socks should be made of some sort of fabric that will wick moisture away. Polypropylene is good; so are nylon, silk, wool, and a whole variety of other choices. Just don't wear cotton. When cotton gets wet, it stays wet.

The outer socks should be something warm and sturdy and resilient. Ragg wool is often the best choice.

GLOVES AND MITTENS: A HANDFUL

Leather, wool, cotton, down, synthetics, and any combination of the above: How do you decide which is best? Again, use your common sense. What will you need them for?

Leather is great for driving or chopping wood, but if it gets wet it stays wet, it's heavy, and can stiffen easily.

Opposite page: Mt. Blanc, France.

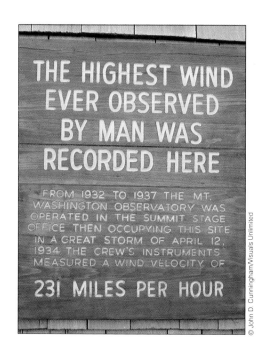

THE HIGHEST WIND EVER OBSERVED BY MAN WAS RECORDED HERE

FROM 1932 TO 1937 THE MT. WASHINGTON OBSERVATORY WAS OPERATED IN THE SUMMIT STAGE OFFICE THEN OCCUPYING THIS SITE IN A GREAT STORM OF APRIL 12, 1934 THE CREW'S INSTRUMENTS MEASURED A WIND VELOCITY OF

231 MILES PER HOUR

Wool and pile are warm and lightweight fabrics, but the wind cuts right through them.

Down is warm but practically useless when wet.

The answer, again, is layering. Wool or pile liners with synthetic mitts are popular, for good reason. Other combinations of warm, water- and wind-repelling fabrics are equally successful.

Mittens are warmer than gloves.

EXTRAS: READ ALL ABOUT THEM

Bandannas

On a recent camping trip we heard one woman comment that she always brings a bandanna with her, but she never uses it. How strange. On that same trip, we used our bandannas as sweatbands, pot holders, handkerchiefs, and sponges. After one of us took a nasty fall on some rocks, a bandanna was a bandage; on other trips, they've been used as tourniquets or to tie a splint to a potentially broken bone.

Moccasins/Sneakers/Booties

Bring along a pair of lightweight shoes to wear around camp. Your feet will thank you for it.

Boot Laces

The most wonderful boots in the world won't do you any good if they won't stay on your feet. Extra laces don't take up much room in your pack, and they can save your trip.

Bathing Suit

Useful not only for the obvious, but for unexpected dips into lakes or streams and for river crossings as well.

Sunglasses

Not a good idea to wear them in deep woods, but sometimes critical for snow, desert, and ridgetop hiking. Don't forget a strap, unless you enjoy chasing your sunglasses down mountain slopes.

© Bob Winsett/Tom Stack & Associates

Beginning your hike in short pants is not a problem, but make sure you bring along the extras: long pants, gloves, hats, socks, etc.

CHAPTER THREE

Camping in Alaska is always a visually fulfilling excursion.

WHAT TO BRING: SHELTER

You've probably made a few trips to your local outdoor store by now, so you've learned the first basic rule of accumulating the gear you want and need: Everything costs a lot—everything you want, that is.

That quickly leads to another rule: Don't rush out and buy everything—borrow or rent until you know exactly what you want. Many of those same places that will be happy to sell you a tent or a pack or a sleeping bag will be just as happy to rent you one. Take advantage of that policy, or ask your friends if you can borrow some of their gear. It's a wonderful way to educate yourself about the merits and demerits of various competing models. styles, and brands so that you can avoid disappointment when you finally do buy.

WHAT TO WEAR

SOMEONE ONCE STARTED THE RUMOR THAT THE APPROPRIATE APPAREL FOR SLEEPING-BAG SLEEPING IS NOTHING AT ALL. YET, WHILE SLEEPING IN THE NUDE MAY BE COMFORTABLE FOR SOME, IT CAN GET CHILLY IN A SLEEPING BAG, JUST AS IT CAN ANYWHERE ELSE. MOST PEOPLE ARE COMFORTABLE IN A T-SHIRT OR LONG JOHNS, GIVE OR TAKE A COUPLE OF OTHER LAYERS. IN COLD WEATHER, MANY CAMPERS WEAR A WOOL CAP. WRAPPING A SWEATER OR JACKET AROUND YOUR NECK TO HELP KEEP YOUR BODY HEAT INSIDE IS ANOTHER WAY TO STAY WARM.

TEMPERATURE RATINGS

ZERO DEGREES IS ZERO DEGREES IS ZERO DEGREES. THAT'S WHAT YOU THINK. YOU KNOW HOW YOU WEAR DIFFERENT SIZE CLOTHES, DEPENDING ON WHICH MANUFACTURER'S GOODS YOU'RE TRYING ON? THE SAME PRINCIPLE IS TRUE WITH TEMPERATURE RATINGS. USE THEM ONLY AS A GENERAL GUIDE. HOW WARM YOU'LL BE DEPENDS ON A LOT OF OTHER FACTORS: YOUR METABOLISM, YOUR TENT (OR LACK THEREOF), WHAT YOU'RE WEARING, AND SO ON.

Use camping-supply store salespeople as a resource. The people who make a living selling gear are often the same people who spend their free time using it. Find a salesperson with your interests. If you've got a specific question about a certain type of backpacking tent, even the best-educated scuba diver or bike rider is going to give you second-hand advice. Find someone who has used the gear you're interested in and who can give you specific advice.

By the way, even though sporting-goods and military-surplus stores do sell much that resembles backpacking gear (and some of it is the genuine thing), you'll do a lot better at a bonafide outdoor store. You'll find more knowledgeable salespeople and a greater selection.

If you know exactly what you want, try checking camping-supply catalogues before buying. Their prices are often quite competitive. (See the appendix for some names and addresses.)

SLEEPING BAGS: IT'S WHAT'S INSIDE THAT COUNTS

If you are going to be sleeping outside in any but the warmest of summer nights, a sleeping bag is one of those "must have" pieces of gear. Some people may curl up inside their parka or make due with a blanket roll or the old bag they used when they were kids, but most of us—especially those of us who are going to be carrying our bag on our backs—quickly awaken to the wonders of the modern lightweight insulated sleeping bag.

Like boots and packs and other hiking gear, sleeping bags now come in a startling array of shapes, sizes, colors, designs, and materials. When you go to a store and see them hanging there in all their intimidating glory, don't panic. If you know what sort of bag you're looking for, you won't be overwhelmed by the choice.

Like parkas and other insulating clothing, a sleeping bag does not create any warmth on its own. What it does do is retain the heat your body creates (very likely to be the only heat available) by trapping as many pockets of air as possible. The more pockets, the more insulation. But, at the same time, the bag can't just conserve the heat until you roast. It's got to have some ventilation, as well. A sleeping bag, like your layers of clothes, must help you achieve "thermal equilibrium"—you should be warm, but not too warm.

What sort of miraculous device can do such a thing? Let's take a bag apart to find out, starting with the fill.

Most people agree that down sleeping bags are the top of the line for a very simple reason: Ounce for ounce, down will keep you warmer than anything else on the market. It will also compress much more tightly than a synthetic fill, making a much less bulky bag to carry around.

If you want a down bag, check the label. Make sure it says down (goose or duck), as opposed to feathers or other materials. State laws require such labels to be attached to the bag.

With the superior performance it conveys, why doesn't everyone buy down? Simple: 1) It's expensive; 2) some people are allergic to it; 3) it's almost useless when wet; and 4) it's hard to dry.

Excellent synthetics are available these days. Cheaper, they'll dry quickly and keep you warm at the same time. These features make many backpackers happy to put up with their relative bulk and weight. You need a scorecard to keep up with the various synthetics on the market; presenting a list here would be useless, for it would be out of date by the time you read it.

Since a sleeping bag—no matter what it's made of—depends on you to warm the air inside, it's critical that you select a bag that fits. You don't want to have to use valuable energy heating up a lot of empty space. That's one reason that mummy bags, which taper at the feet and usually have a hood and collar, are the most popular. If the bag fits you right, there's not much excess room for you to heat. The downside is that what's snug and comfortable for one person may induce claustrophobia in another.

So some people prefer a roomy rectangular shape. They figure that extra elbow room is worth the extra weight. Rectangular bags can be great on warm nights, since they have a wide, open mouth and a zipper that can be zipped open (or closed) all the way around. Semirectangular bags are just what they sound like: a compromise, offering some of the roominess of the rectangular shape, without all its weight.

It's not easy to lie down and get into a sleeping bag in the middle of a store, but it is really important that you try your bag on before you buy it. You don't want to find out that it doesn't fit when you're out in the wilderness and there's absolutely nothing you can do to remedy the situation.

The bag's shell is, of course, also critical. If you're getting down fill, check out the waterproof, breathable shells on the market—the further expense may be justified. Otherwise, nylon or another synthetic can be fine. Just look for durability, good construction, and a comfortable feeling against your skin.

DOWN DOWNHILL

SOME PEOPLE FROM THE THEY-DON'T-MAKE-'EM-LIKE-THEY-USED-TO CONTINGENT SAY THAT THE QUALITY OF DOWN HAS GONE DOWNHILL. DOWN IS A BYPRODUCT OF BIRDS THAT ARE SLAUGHTERED FOR FOOD. WHILE YOUNG BIRDS ARE BEST FOR EATING, THE ONES WITH THE BEST DOWN ARE FULL GROWN; VERY FEW COMMERCIAL DOWN-PRODUCING BIRDS LIVE LONG ENOUGH TO PROVIDE THE ULTIMATE QUALITY DOWN.

Courtesy of Recreational Equipment Inc.

Ask yourself when you are going to be using the bag, and buy the appropriate one. But remember: Better to be too warm than not warm enough.

How a sleeping bag's fill should be managed depends on what that fill is. Down, which tends to flow almost like a liquid, would quickly get pushed away from the heaviest parts of the body if it weren't forced to stay put by the bag's construction. Therefore, the down is stuffed into a series of tubes that restrict its movement, and these tubes are stitched together to create the bag. Tubes that run across the bag are a lot more effective than those that run up and down its length.

The problem with these tubes is that everywhere their stitches lie, down doesn't. No matter how warm the down, if it alternates with uninsulated stitched stripes the bag isn't going to be very warm. So manufacturers have come up with various systems, with slanting the tubes' walls (baffles) probably being the best.

Synthetic-fill bags are easier to make, since synthetics don't move around as easily as down. But do look for "edge-stabilized" bags, in which the edge of the insulation is sewn securely to the shell.

Check the zipper. Make sure it's sturdy and easy to use (in some models, the zipper tends to eat right into the fabric of the bag). Two-way zippers can provide great ventilation in warm weather. Also, remember that many bags can be "mated," so that you can create one big sleeping bag for the two of you. If you'll want to do this, make sure your bags' zippers are compatible, and also make sure the bags zip on opposite sides. (If your zippers don't mate and you'd like them to, ask at an outdoor store about a gizmo you can buy that offers instant matability.) Also check that there's an insulated flap over the zipper to prevent heat loss, and always remember: All other things being equal, the shorter the zipper, the warmer the bag.

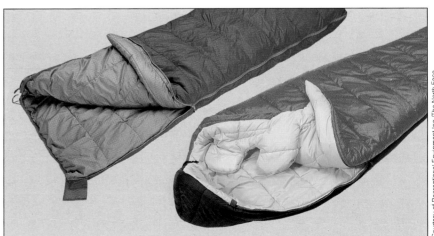

Courtesy of Recreational Equipment Inc./The North Face

Finally, ask yourself when you are going to be using the bag. If you're a warm-weather camper, a lightweight, low-cost bag may do you fine. But don't underestimate your needs if you're planning to be sleeping outside in cold weather. Better to be too warm than not warm enough.

LINERS: INTERIORS

A dirty sleeping bag is not only smelly and unpleasant, but it won't keep you as warm. One way to keep it clean is to use a washable liner (made of flannel or other lightweight material).

Other liners, intended for extra warmth, are made of various sorts of space-age stuff. Inserted into a sleeping bag, they can keep you ten degrees (or more) warmer. They're popular because they work hard, weigh little, and take up hardly any room at all.

PADS: THE GROUND STORY

The main problem with sleeping on the ground is that the ground has two main sleep-inhibiting attributes: It's cold, and it's hard. Therefore, for our convenience, we have pads.

There are air mattresses, closed-cell foam pads, open-cell foam pads, and the famous Therm-a-Rest mattresses.

Air mattresses can be comfortable (remember not to inflate them all the way), but they puncture easily and don't provide much insulation between you and the ground.

Foam pads—inexpensive, durable, and lightweight—are not the most comfortable of choices, but they serve. For years, they've been the budget backpacker's favorite pad. Closed-cell foam is lighter, less bulky, and more waterproof than its open-cell cousin (the one that often has bumps like those on egg cartons). But open-cell foam can be more comfortable.

Today's mattress of choice, however, is the best of both worlds, the Therm-a-Rest, an open-cell foam pad covered with a waterproof airtight fabric shell. Open the valve at one corner, and these mattresses self-inflate to create a wonderfully comfortable insulated surface to sleep on. They're lightweight, compact, and long-lasting, but they don't come cheap. Most backpackers say the comfort justifies the expense, and they buy the hip-length model unless extreme cold calls for the additional cost and weight of the full-length model. You certainly get what you pay for here.

Opposite page: Choose the bag that suits you.

Courtesy of Recreational Equipment Inc./Therm-a-Rest

For sleeping on air, Therm-a-Rest mattresses are best.

WITH A LITTLE SKILL AND A LOT OF NYLON ROPE, YOU CAN KEEP YOURSELF AND YOUR GEAR DRY AND WARM USING A FLAT SHEET OF PLASTIC, A FLY, OR A TARP WITH EDGE GROMMETS.

Another layer between you and the ground is the groundsheet. Aside from affording additional insulation, it will protect your sleeping bag or tent floor from puncture and invasion by insects and water.

Coated nylon tarps certainly do the trick, as does plain plastic sheeting—the kind that painters use as dropcloths.

Adding an extra layer or two of almost anything between you and the ground is a great way to stay warm—or get warm—especially in frigid weather. Try using your jacket, a sweater, or a few sheets of newspaper (if you happen to bring any along).

HAMMOCKS: ON AIR

Though some people claim they'll never be able to sleep in a hammock, others swear there's nothing better on those hot summer nights. Note that mosquito netting for hammocks is available and might be called for on those same hot summer nights.

Hammocks can be handy in places where there are scorpions and snakes. Some kids love them. They're also great for stashing food and gear.

The best thing about them is they're lightweight: Sleep in a hammock and you don't need to lug a sleeping bag and tent along.

TENTS: I THINK WE'RE NOT IN CANVAS ANYMORE

Why in the world do we go to all the trouble of selecting, preparing, and packing everything we need for a backpacking trip and then carry it all on our backs all day, just to arrive at a campsite, pitch a tent, climb in, and zip the door up tight?

There does seem to be an inherent contradiction in backpacking with a tent. If the whole point of the trip in the first place is to be outside, why don't we sleep outside, too?

Sleeping outside permits us to see the nighttime world. Without a tent to make a large blot on the landscape, we may go unnoticed by small animals or birds, and be able to watch them going about their business unalarmed by our presence. Without a roof over our heads, we can see the sun rise and set, and watch the changing patterns of the stars.

Without a tent, we also leave ourselves open to other types of experiences: Rain. Cold. Scorpions. Lack of privacy. Dew. Snow. Mosquitoes. Insomnia.

So—we have the tent, if not absolutely necessary at all times, a handy item to have with you when planning to sleep outdoors.

TYPES OF TENTS

Everyone knows (in fact, most of us have owned) the traditional *A-frame tent*. They're sturdy, easy to set up, and—usually—relatively inexpensive. A-frames are often the tent of choice of experienced outdoorspeople heading into a challenging situation: These tents cope easily with wind, rain, and snow.

But they're kind of cramped inside. *Hoop tents* and *dome tents* offer much more spacious living quarters and especially more headroom, but their design is perhaps not as stable in high winds, and some people complain about their performance in the rain.

The *bivouac sack* is an answer to the question "What's a good lightweight tent that has enough room for one person and no gear and would be comfortable in warm weather?" A bivouac sack—kind of a glorified sleeping bag cover with a mesh head section—will keep moisture and bugs out while weighing in at only a couple of pounds.

For winter camping, you'll need a tent that goes up quickly and easily, and then will stay up under the force of heavy winds and the weight of a load of wet snow. It has to be big enough to fit you and all your gear, and it has to vent easily without letting flying snow join you inside.

There are various types of huge *family-style tents* suitable for car-camping at campgrounds. They're well ventilated, comfortable, and spacious—but then, so is a house. These tents—some of which weight up to sixty pounds—are not made for backpacking.

FEATURES

Put a warm body or two inside a nylon enclosure, zip it closed, and you're going to get humidity on the inside. Add some rain, snow, or dew, and you've got humidity on the top. Then there's the dampness from the ground or rain run-off coming in from below. A good tent has to keep all this wetness out.

A standard way of approaching the problem is with the double-walled tent—that is, a tent that is made of some sturdy waterproofed material below and part of the way up the wall (a "bathtub" bottom) and some porous, breathable material above, all topped with an optional (or sometimes, permanent) waterproof fly.

SEW A NYLON LOOP INSIDE YOUR TENT AT EACH END OF THE ROOF. YOU CAN CLIP LIGHTS TO THESE LOOPS OR ATTACH A ROPE TO SERVE AS A CLOTHESLINE FOR SMALL ITEMS LIKE SOCKS, WHICH CAN DRY OVERNIGHT.

Camping in Iceland.

MOST TENTS COME WITH LIGHT METAL STAKES, WHICH ARE FINE IN SOFT SOIL. BUT JUST TRY TO USE THEM IN SAND OR SNOW. THE FIRST THING MANY PEOPLE DO WHEN THEY BUY A NEW TENT IS REPLACE THESE STAKES WITH METAL OR PLASTIC STAKES AT LEAST SIX INCHES LONG. IF YOU DO THIS, JUST MAKE SURE THE NEW STAKES FIT THROUGH THE LOOPS IN YOUR TENT.

With the advent of breathable waterproof materials, the single-walled tent is making a comeback.

Look for a tent with plenty of ventilation, and make sure that it is possible to zip each and every one of the windows closed.

While mesh netting is ubiquitous in tents these days, some people caution that some mesh is too big to keep tiny biting insects (no-see-ums) out. Consider yourself warned.

Check the zippers on the doors. Make sure they open from the top. With these, you can get some air in while keeping rain and snow out. Also check to see that all exposed zippers are covered with rain flaps.

HOW DO YOU CHOOSE?

There is no best tent. In fact, there is no best type of tent. You must examine your plans, explore your options, and ask a lot of questions before you make a decision.

Remember that the words "season" and "man" (or "person") when used to rate a tent are highly subjective. The first, usually prefaced by "three-" or "four-" is indicative only of a tent's relative strengths. An inexperienced camper in a four-season tent caught unaware in a summer shower might have substantially more problems than another in an early-winter blizzard with a summer-mesh tent and years of experience.

The size of a tent is also relative. If you and your companion are stuck inside a two-person tent with all your gear during a three-day monsoon, you'll likely be cursing the designer, the manufacturer, and each other before it's all over. Consider the relative comfort that extra room can bring, and measure it against the extra weight.

If you feel the tent you have is too small, consider buying only a vestibule to add space instead of a whole new tent.

When you go to the store to check out their tents, make sure you actually climb inside each and every one you're considering buying. Examine the quality of the manufacture—inside and out—and practice pitching the tent and taking it down before you buy. Be alert to design flaws and complicated procedures. Women especially seem to have a problem with some A-frames' ridgepoles; be sure you don't buy a tent you can't use by yourself.

When you've found the tent you want, see if you can rent it first. Take it out for a test drive before you spend the money.

This tent is nestled comfortably within view of the night sky over Creston Needle, Colorado.

© Spencer Swanger/Tom Stack & Associates

CHAPTER FOUR

© Spencer Swanger/Tom Stack & Associates

HOW TO BRING IT: PACKS

You might have the most comfortable boots, the roomiest tent, and the most efficient stove ever made, but—pure and simple—you are going to hate backpacking if your backpack isn't up to par.

Your backpack is your all-important lifeline, but it can also be the bane of your existence.

The wrong pack will give you sore shoulders and an aching back, and when, thirty miles from nowhere, you get so frustrated that you give it a good kick, it will simply give up and die.

So, before you go, you should be sure you know not only how to pick it, fit it, and pack it, but also how to fix it if it breaks.

DON'T HANG HEAVY ITEMS ON THE OUT-SIDE OF THE PACK BAG, ESPECIALLY ON AN INTERNAL-FRAME PACK.

THROW IN A FEW EXTRA PLASTIC BAGS. YOU CAN NEVER HAVE TOO MANY OF THEM—FOR STORAGE, FOR PACKING, FOR KEEPING THE WET FROM THE DRY AND THE SMELLY FROM THE RELATIVELY ODOR-FREE. JUST DON'T DROP THE BAGS ON THE TRAIL OR ABANDON THEM AT YOUR CAMPSITE WHEN YOU LEAVE.

TRY PERIODICALLY SHIFTING THE WEIGHT OF THE PACK FROM THE HIP BELT TO THE SHOULDER STRAPS TO PROVIDE TEMPORARY RELIEF TO ACHING MUSCLES.

THE ANATOMY OF A PACK

We don't know who invented the backpack, but we do know what one early innovation looked like: A big bag with a strap—called a tump line—that went across your forehead. You stuffed everything inside, put your head through the strap, and then let your neck muscles do all the work.

While tump lines are still used in Africa, Nepal, and other places where people have very strong necks, most of us have embraced the shoulder-strap version—with the addition of a relatively recent innovation, the hip belt. Introduced around 1960, the padded hip belt transfers most of the pack's weight from the relatively weak (especially in women) muscles of the upper body to the powerful hips and legs. The more padding, the more comfortable the belt will be. (Be sure, though, that it's not so bulky that it gets in your way when you move.)

Hip belts should buckle securely and be adjustable enough to fit you well, regardless of the number of layers of clothing you are wearing at the time. They should also be easy to get out of in an emergency; the comfort of a well-fitting hip belt will be more than cancelled by the discomfort and danger you'll feel as you're being swept down a stream unable to release yourself from your pack's grasp.

Shoulder straps, which keep the pack close to the body as well as support some of the weight, should also be well padded, solidly constructed, and adjustable. They should attach to each other in the front with sternum straps which, once adjusted for your body—no small task, especially for women—will help shift more weight away from the shoulders.

All these straps are intended to attach your body to the other two parts of the pack: the bag and the frame.

The bag, obviously, is where all your stuff goes. It comes in various sizes. Since the bag must contain every single thing you'll need to have with you, it has got to be roomy, but be sure you need—and will be able to maneuver with—all the space you are buying.

Bags can open at the top or zip all the way around. If you're very organized and can anticipate your needs for the day when you pack, you may be able to cope with a top-loading bag that permits little fumbling around to find things. (Top-loaders, which are tied closed, have other plusses—having no zipper, they're usually more waterproof, and you don't have to worry about your zipper breaking.)

They should have a few compartments to help you organize your gear, and boast plentiful outside pockets as well. Lastly—does this even need to be emphasized?—they should be made of a strong, durable, water-resistant fabric that is reinforced at key areas. The fabric will have to put up with dirt, water, rocks, and any one of a whole range of other challenges. It must be up to the job.

Then there's the frame, the part of the pack that is the subject of the most—in fact, endless—debate. Internal or external?—the question of the ages.

External-frame packs came first, the idea behind them being to lift the bag's weight up off the shoulders and, with the help of the hip belt, place it squarely on the hips. These frames are what most people think of when they think "backpack"—big, rectangular metal (usually aluminum) frames on the outside of the bag and shoulder straps and hip belt to provide support.

Packs with internal frames—usually nothing more than a pair of thin, strong, flexible metal strips embedded in the pack's back—are more recent innovations. Usually smaller and narrower, they are somewhat flexible and sit more closely to the body.

So how do you decide which one's for you? It's a personal decision, and you'll find as many devout supporters of one as you will of the other.

But there are some basic guidelines to follow. You'll probably do better with an internal-frame pack if you tend to go backpacking in places a plane flight away from home (they hold up much better under baggage-handler abuse); if you're going to carry your pack on skis or snowshoes or while climbing (they make a cleaner line and interfere less with your balance); or if you're going to be hiking through dense brush (ditto). Women, especially short, small boned-women, often find that internal-frame packs fit them better than external-frame models. On the other hand, external-frame packs tend to be bigger and more capable of coping with heavy loads (the right choice for long or cold-weather treks when you'll need a lot of gear) and cooler (they don't hug your back as closely).

All that aside, the paramount factor in your decision-making should be fit.

FITTING THE PACK

Finding a pack that fits poses many of the same problems as finding the right pair of boots. Since pack manufacturers design their products to fit a certain specific body type, if you do not have that body type it will probably not be

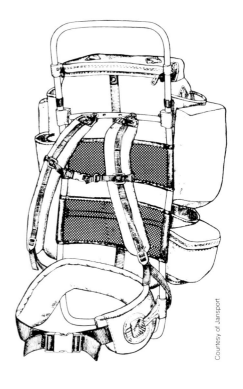

External-frame pack.

Internal-frame pack.

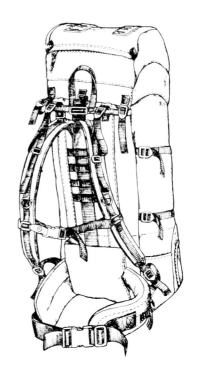

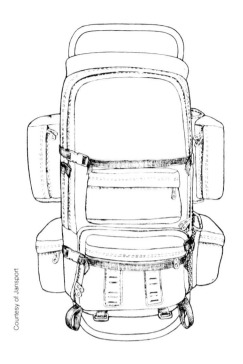

Courtesy of Jansport

External-frame pack.

Courtesy of Jansport

Typical daypack.

easy to find a pack that will fit you. True, packs are adjustable, but not infinitely so. So try on as many models as necessary until you find one that feels right.

Start with the frame size. The smaller your torso, the smaller the frame you should have, and vice versa. Many manufacturers produce packs in a few sizes, so don't even consider settling for the wrong one. The straps should connect to the frame at or slightly above shoulder level, not below.

Once you've put the pack on, have someone dump some weight (at least twenty pounds) inside. Then adjust the shoulder straps and hip belt—paying extremely close attention to the manufacturer's instructions and the advice of a knowledgeable salesperson—and take a hike around the store. How do your shoulders, hips, and back feel? There should be no discomfort. If the straps dig into any part of your anatomy or the pack develops a swagger of its own under these circumstances, imagine how it'll feel after a day of carrying forty pounds. You don't have to settle for an uncomfortable pack, and a responsible outfitter should be willing to work with you until it's right.

Once you've found the pack that feels it was made with you in mind, see if you can rent it and take it for a test hike. Most reliable outfitters will allow you to do that. Packs aren't cheap; you really don't want to buy one until you're sure it's right.

PACK PACKING

Some experienced hikers say it doesn't make a difference how you pack your pack—as long as you've got everything you need and nothing sharp is sticking into your back. But most adhere to the tradition of packing heavy things up high and in close to your back, with the lighter ones below and outside, especially with an external-frame pack. (With an internal-frame pack, it's less important for the weight to be up high than it is for it to be in close to your body.) The explanation goes that since the top of a pack tends to tilt slightly forward, it—and its heavy contents—lies over the strong muscles of your hips and legs, right where you want the weight to be.

All of which is fine if you're walking on a relatively well-maintained trail with only moderate slopes. But if you're going to be contending with steep inclines and rough terrain, think about another approach to packing. Try putting all the heavy stuff below, with the light things perched up on high. Having a lower center of balance will increase your stability.

Scrunch your clothes up and stuff them in the pack. They'll take less space this way, and don't worry about wrinkles—they'll all disappear and, after all, who's going to notice.

Also, remember that those compression straps are there for a reason. The tighter you cinch them, the closer the pack's weight will be to your body. And if you have a front-loading pack, the straps will take some pressure off the zipper, thereby giving the zipper a longer life.

OTHER TYPES OF PACKS

If you're going to take dayhikes—from home or from your base camp—you'll want to have a small pack. *Daypacks* need no introduction—they're on the back of practically every student you see. They come in sizes small to large, in materials from nylon to suede, in neutral colors and day-glo hues that will stand out in any crowd, not to mention the woods.

The hard part isn't deciding whether or not you need one (you probably do, if you don't have one already), but it's finding the one you need among all the choices.

First decide how big a bag you need. You'll be carrying an extra sweater or jacket, lunch, a first-aid kit, and a water bottle, in addition to your maps, field guides, binoculars, and so on. Then check the packs you think are right for construction. Are the seams well made? Are the zippers sturdy? Are the shoulder straps sewn securely to the pack itself?

Look for a bag with padded shoulder straps, a nice plus for comfort. Some even have padded backs, which are comfortable, but tend to be too warm on summer days. Hip straps, third cousins to hip belts, do actually help keep some weight off the shoulders.

And be sure to try the pack on. Various designs fit various people in various ways. Find a model that's right for you. Be comfortable with the color, too. Remember you'll be taking the pack into the country or to the top of a mountain, not a fashion show.

We've recently discovered the joys of fanny packs, another option for short hikes. There's nothing like the feeling of getting the weight off your shoulders and back, and putting it right where those big muscles are. Fanny packs start small, with about enough room to stash a map and compass, but there are plenty of models that can handle almost as much as the average daypack yet still be considered a fanny pack.

Mt. Washington, New Hampshire.

© Robert Winslow

At the Grand Canyon: Sometimes a fanny pack is all you need.

A couple of manufacturers have recently come out with a new breed of backpack that ostensibly offers the best of both worlds. Operating on the theory that you should carry only as much pack as you need, it is made of a daypack or fanny pack zipped to a few compartments of various shapes and sizes. Take only what you need when you need it.

Then there are travel packs, or soft packs, convertible sofas of the backpack family. With a zip here and a buckle there, these bags can magically transform from innocent-looking carry-on luggage, able to contend with any airline-induced atrocity with aplomb, to a pretty good backpack. Of course, these backpacks aren't as well designed as regular ones, but they do allow you to switch from city slickness to country comfort with unsurpassed speed.

PACK CARE

Abrasion is the mortal enemy of the backpack. Dirt causes abrasion, so try to keep your pack as clean as possible. Make sure no rocks or sticks get inside, and protect it from being poked by tent poles or other sharp objects. Make sure you clean it—even wash it with mild soap if necessary—at the end of the season to ensure its durability.

Just because an external frame is a tough and durable pack support doesn't mean that it's tough and durable for anything else. Sitting on a frame, not to mention using it as a ladder or other tool, can easily break it. In camp, your pack should be propped up against a tree, not left lying on the ground.

It's wise to waterproof your pack and to seal the seams. If you're heading out to a rain forest or expect to be crossing a lot of streams, it's even wiser to waterproof everything inside the pack by stuffing it into a series of plastic bags. Stuffing a stuff sack into a plastic bag and then putting the whole thing into another stuff sack will further ensure that the fragile waterproof layer will be protected.

BEFORE YOU HIT THE TRAIL, BE SURE YOU KNOW HOW YOUR EQUIPMENT WORKS. CAN YOU TAKE EVERYTHING APART AND PUT IT BACK TOGETHER? CAN YOU FIX IT IF IT BREAKS?

If At First You Don't Succeed

So you're fit and you're ready. You know where you're going, and what you're taking with you. You've got a great pack, and you know how to stash your gear inside it. So pack it up, put the whole load on your back—and off you go.

Not so fast.

If anyone has ever set off just like that their first time out, we'd like to know. Most people, once they've felt the weight of their fully loaded pack for the first time take it right off their backs, sit down, and do some serious thinking. Those who conclude that they're not crazy for even thinking about going backpacking open their packs up, dump everything out, and throw every item they don't consider totally vital as far across the room as possible.

Once you're past this point, you really are ready to go.

A pack that has been properly fitted can help you shoulder even the heaviest load.

Walking with a Pack

If you've never walked with a fully loaded pack before, the main rule is to take it easy. Do not expect to be able to eat up the miles at the same rate you do on an afternoon's dayhike or a stroll around the neighborhood. That sounds obvious, but there are a lot of people out there who have suffered because of a too-fast pace. Walk with an easy stride, without turning your feet in or out or raising your knees too high. Try to establish a rhythm and stick with it.

Come to terms with the fact that people of varying leg lengths and abilities and ages will likely move at different rates. If you know where you're going

and you agree where to meet, don't feel that members of a group must stick together at all times.

Lean forward a little if it helps, especially going uphill.

Try to walk quietly so as not to intrude on nature's quiet, and avoid stepping on any delicate greenery you might encounter at the trail's side. If you find a stick or rock forcing water onto a trail, remove it. Tread lightly at all times, especially in fragile areas.

Avoid stepping on rocks or branches to avoid twisting your ankle or knee. Remember, you won't be as agile as usual with a pack on your back.

BREAK TIME

Don't forget to take lots of breaks—short ones with your pack on, long ones with your pack off, luxurious ones with your boots off, too, and your feet in a cool stream. Many hikers feel that one break every forty-five minutes or so is the minimum, giving them the endurance to last all day.

The other thing about breaks is that they give you the opportunity to relax, look around, and take in the view. Hiking—with your eyes on the trail at all times—can get you places, but unless you stop and look around, you won't even see where you've been. Remember that one of the pleasures of backpacking is to see remote vistas and glory in natural surroundings mostly untouched and unseen by other people.

THIRD LEG

A walking stick will certainly help with stability. Once you get used to carrying one, you won't believe you ever did without, especially over rough terrain. But they're a big help with just plain walking, too, somehow almost pushing you along with pendulum-like motion. They're invaluable when crossing a stream, negotiating a rocky or icy slope, or convincing hungry raccoons, maybe even a bear, that your food is not for them.

Walking sticks can be found (usually there's a good supply of abandoned ones near any trailhead), made (of anything from elegantly carved fine wood to a broomstick to aluminum tubing), or bought (take a look at the ads in the back of an outdoor magazine for a sample).

On the theory that more is more, a few innovative hikers use two sticks—adapted ski poles, actually. A telescoping model is on the market, able to be stashed safely in your pack when you don't need it.

A hiker in Silver Falls Park, Oregon, takes a minute to replenish his energy and take in some fall colors.

CHAPTER FIVE

© W. Banaszewski/Visuals Unlimited

WHAT TO BRING:
FOOD AND COOKING

This is a test. At the end of a long day on the trail, the average backpacker is (A) ravenous, (B) starving, (C) dying of hunger, or (D) all of the above. If you picked (D), you pass.

Backpackers are a hungry bunch, and with good reason: Backpacking is hard work. Your body will burn substantially more fuel carrying a heavy load all day than it will when you're at home planning your trip.

While you'll undoubtedly lose some weight on a strenuous trek (unless you're one of those few who manage to get in top condition before the trip,

THE ALUMINIM POUCHES THAT HOLD BACK-
PACKING FOOD MAY PROTECT THE FOOD,
BUT THEY'RE NO GOOD FOR THE ENVIRON-
MENT. REMEMBER TO PACK THEM OUT.
USED PACKAGES CAN OCCASIONALLY
COME IN HANDY TO HOLD OTHER ITEMS OR
EVEN AS DRINKING CUPS.

PEANUT BUTTER, THOUGH A RELATIVE
HEAVYWEIGHT, IS HIGH IN PROTEIN, FATS,
AND CARBOHYDRATES, MAKING IT A GOOD
HIKER'S SNACK.

the way we're all supposed to), don't plan on doing it by cutting back on your calorie intake. In fact, plan on consuming perhaps twice as many calories on the trail as you do at home. Some suggest that an average of a whopping four thousand calories per person per day (depending, of course, on the person) is not too much. In cold weather, where more energy is expended, the total should be around six thousand.

The majority of these calories (about 60 percent) should derive from carbohydrates, which is pretty much the way doctors and nutritionists have been telling us to eat for years anyway. Pack plenty of pasta, grains, flour, dried fruit, and nuts. The sugars in these foods will be metabolized quickly and give you a quick energy boost, but the complex carbos in pastas and grains will burn slowly for hours, keeping you warm through the night or giving you the energy for a long hike.

Proteins, which rebuild body tissues, take even longer to metabolize, so the energy they provide is even longer lasting. Milk, cheese, meat, fish, legumes, and grains are all good protein sources. Some people feel that proteins make them feel sluggish and slow them down, so consider avoiding a big protein-rich dinner the night before a long, hard hike.

While many of us try to avoid eating fats at home, outdoor athletes often seek them out—in the form of nuts, cheese, meat, chocolate, oil, margarine, and butter—for their high-calorie content, especially in cold weather.

Since some people never leave home without a few bottles of vitamins, they'll certainly take them along on the trails. But there's a pretty powerful school of thought that says that if you eat right—everything in moderation—you'll more than satisfy your requirement for vitamins and minerals, both at home and in the woods.

WORTH ITS WEIGHT

Backpacking food must meet other criteria beyond nutrition, of course. It's also got to be lightweight, easy to prepare, and able to last practically forever without refrigeration. Good taste is nice too, but we'll come to that later.

Since they can't pack all of their favorite meals, the food most backpackers bring on trips is something that comes out of a package in an arid form that, when mixed with water and sometimes cooked, is famous for taking on a glutinous consistency and a suspiciously chemical flavor. But it is lightweight, easy to prepare, and long-lasting.

When confronted with the typical slop-food jokes, backpacking-food manufacturers hasten to assure us that no, no, their products aren't like that anymore—that's the way it used to be—times have changed. And, the fact is, at least to a degree, they are right: Freeze-dried food has come a long way. Many people who swore off the stuff a decade ago are coming back to it and finding that it's not so bad after all. Some even actually like it.

The manufacturers do have a problem. How do you take a serving of turkey tetrazzini, place it in a vacuum, freeze it, remove the ice, seal the rest in an aluminum pouch, and have anyone believe that what you end up with actually has anything to do with turkey tetrazzini?

There's also dehydrated food, much of which you can find in a supermarket (or your own shelves). Powdered soup, potatoes, puddings, fruit drinks, milk, and so on fall into this category. Once a food has been dehydrated (usually by boiling and boiling it and then exposing it to heat), it bears little resemblance to its original form, even less than freeze-dried food does. But it does fit the three requirements of trail food.

One big change in backpacking food in the last few years is that most manufacturers have cut down on their use of salt, MSG, preservatives, and other artificial additives. A few even make a conscious effort to prepare only whole foods with organic ingredients. There's also a much wider choice of food to select from—the cuisine of practically every ethnic group is represented in freeze-dried form, and there are almost as many choices for vegetarians now as there are for carnivores.

Dry It Yourself

One big problem that many backpackers have with commercially prepared food—even those who like the way it tastes—is how much it costs. So some dehydrate their own food.

In theory, there are no limits to the foods that can be dehydrated: Fruit, vegetables, canned fish and meat, grains, beans, sauces, and soups have all been successfully dried at home. People suggest that cooking grains and beans at home before drying them saves cooking time on the trail. They also caution that fruits and vegetables should be blanched first to help preserve them safely.

Health-food stores are a good source of information on home drying, and many sell dehydrators as well.

© Matt Bradley/Tom Stack & Associates

Mealtime in Hot Springs National Park, Arkansas.

GOURMET ON THE GO

Some backpackers turn their noses up at freeze-dried food, saying that they simply won't eat anything outdoors that they wouldn't eat at home.

Indeed, for those who look for them, there are many lightweight "gourmet" items in supermarkets and specialty stores these days. They don't necessarily come cheap, and they do require a bit of imagination and flexibility, but they can make the difference between delight at having a meal and having a delightful meal.

Dried mushrooms can be added to soups, stews, or grains; instant couscous is a delicious substitute for rice; and a small packet of homemade frozen pesto will dress up a bowl of pasta.

FISHING AND GATHERING

There are those backpackers who, going back to nature, want to live off it. If you're out in the wilderness, they say, food is all around you. You can gather it on the beach and in the woods. Even the desert has food to offer. You just have to learn to see it.

The first step is to get yourself a few good field guides from your local outfitter or book store. These will help you find the food you're looking for, tell it apart from poisonous look-alikes, and give you other information (often recipes or bits of lore) to boot.

The danger of gathering wild food, of course, is that it's easy to make a dangerous, if not fatal, error. Therefore, always follow rule number one of wild food gathering: Never eat any plant you cannot positively identify. If there is the slightest suspicion in your mind that the plant you want to eat might actually be its poisonous cousin, just say no. (Some outdoor survival manuals do detail a method of field-testing for poisonous plants. We have no personal experience with this method, and we report it here simply as further evidence of how careful you really must be. First, be sure you have no choice other than to sample an unknown plant: You have no other potential food sources, and you haven't eaten in days and don't expect to in the near future. Then, if you feel you must, chew a small spoonful's worth of this plant and hold it in your mouth for five minutes. If you notice any burning sensation or unpleasant taste, spit it out, and don't try again. Otherwise, swallow it and wait eight hours. If you've suffered no adverse effects, go through the same procedure with a whole mouthful. If, eight more hours later, you're still okay, then, the

Camping next to a fresh stream, lake, or river will surely provide you with a fresh meal for dinner.

books say, the food is *probably* safe to eat.) By this time, even the most bitter tasting plants will taste good to you.

In cases other than life-and-death, though, armed with knowledge and a ravenous appetite, stop for a moment to consider the morality of eating wild plants. If you're in a national park or other wilderness area, you're living in a world where "take only photographs, leave only footprints" is the rule. Don't harvest a thing. Elsewhere, where the rules are looser, consider the integrity of the environment you're in. If a fragile slope depends on its vegetation to avoid erosion, don't pick or trample the plants. If the plant you'd like to taste is rare in the area, leave it be; better to select something that grows abundantly. And even then, take only as much as you'll actually eat. Try to pick leaves and fronds only—leave the plant intact.

The same philosophy holds for backpacking fishermen. While there's little more delicious than a fresh-caught pan-fried trout (particularly after days of preserved food), don't fish out of season. Make sure you've got a local fishing license, or you may find your trout to be the most expensive fish you've ever eaten. And don't take more than local laws allow. Those laws are there for a reason. If you're going to gather shellfish, make sure you have up-to-date information on local red tides and pollution problems. If you're not sure of the condition of the water, stay away. Even the finest clams and oysters aren't worth the risk.

Noshing

Another strategy to cope with mealtime hunger is to prevent the worst of it by snacking all day. If you nibble as you go, you'll also keep your level of energy high when you need it most.

The classic hiker's snack is, of course, gorp, which originally stood for Good Old Raisins and Peanuts, but now means practically any combination of nuts, seeds, dried fruits, and candy. Most hikers opt to create their own mix, turning up their noses at the high cost of supermarket-brand gorp. Everyone has their own favorite combination, M&M candies being perhaps the most popular ingredient.

In Your Cupboard

Regardless of your preferred style of backpacking cuisine, don't forget to pack the staples.

> SNACK AS YOU GO. PACK NOSHABLES IN CONVENIENT EASY-TO-REACH PLACES—A BELT PACK, A SIDE POCKET OF YOUR BACKPACK—SO YOU DON'T HAVE TO STOP AND UNLOAD EVERY TIME YOU WANT A BITE TO EAT.

The snack, a good excuse to take a break and enjoy the view.

There's not much you can do if you crave a fresh green salad when you've been out on the trail for a few days, but, with a little planning, you can have sprouts. Put a small handful of lentils, alfalfa, mung, or soy beans in a wide-mouth plastic container and soak them in water overnight. Then drain them out, and don't forget to rinse them often. Within a few days you'll have sprouts galore, a refreshing snack, and a nice complement to whatever else is on the menu.

Always pack the staples, such as grains, beans, and pastas, as these will form the basis of most of your meals.

Experience points the way to the value of bringing a few little containers of herbs and spices with you. A change in seasoning can bring welcome variety to a menu that looks suspiciously close to the one served at the last meal . . . and the one before that. Try oregano, basil, onion powder, salt (or salt substitute), pepper, curry powder, chili powder, garlic salt, etc., which all work well with a variety of foods. And don't forget a little cinnamon, which can fancy up coffee or tea and make hot chocolate a special treat.

Sugar, like salt, occurs bountifully in many prepared foods, so many people don't choose to add it in additional quantities. But do bring some. It will give you a short-term energy boost if you need it. When carried in the form of candy (slow-melting bittersweet chocolate and hard candies are many backpackers' favorites), it's a popular trail snack.

Lightweight and sturdy plastic tubs—or, better, tubes—of margarine are a big hit with many backpackers. But margarine, while it lasts a lot longer than butter, won't stay fresh too long in the heat. If you're taking an extended summertime hike, look for packages of clarified butter, ghee, which isn't too tasty unheated, but is great for cooking.

Powdered milk is available in versions with varying fat content. You have to decide for yourself how to handle the cholesterol question, but remember that a backpacking trip is not the place for a low-calorie, low-fat diet.

Lightweight, versatile, and easy to pack, grains, beans, and pastas will probably form the basis of most of your meals. Instant cereals are much easier to cook, but not as nutritious as the real thing.

Supermarket casserole mixes are just as good campside as they are at home. Before you buy, check to see what additional ingredients, if any, they require.

Dried soup mixes are plentiful, lightweight, reasonably healthy—a backpacking classic. Whether used to make gravy, as the base for a stew, or even for soup, they're used, and used often. Many hikers consume more soup on a weeklong backpacking trip than they do during the whole rest of the year.

One oft-craved item that backpackers mention is a tall glass of ice-cold, fresh-squeezed orange juice. Dehydrated cold drink mixes have come a long way, but they haven't quite pinned down that fresh-squeezed taste. Just plain water can get awfully boring. Plus, you may want to use these powders to disguise the taste of water that may be safe to drink but hard to stomach. Various concoctions advertise their abilities to replace chemicals the body loses while sweating, something else to consider.

There's nothing like a hot drink first thing in the morning, last thing at night, or anytime you need some comfort or warmth. A good selection of tea, coffee, Ovaltine, and hot chocolate (get the type with milk powder already in it) can make the difference. Hot water with honey and lemon juice or a little cold drink mix is another soothing alternative.

BEFORE YOU GO

There are a few more things you can do at home to make your backpacking meals more pleasant.

The first is to take a long, hard look at all the food you've carefully assembled for your trip. Are you sure there's enough? A hungry hiker is a cranky hiker, and a hungry hiker with no food reserves is potentially in a lot of trouble if an accident occurs.

Then, take a look at how much it's all going to weigh, and say good-bye to all the nice packages the food came home from the store in. Repack everything you can into plastic food containers, bags, and tubes. (This doesn't go for freeze-dried food, which must stay in its foil pouch.) Measure out only the amount of spices, instant coffee, and so on that you'll need. Remove all excess material from the packages. Get rid of heavy glass and metal containers that you're just going to have to pack out anyway. Find an alternate, lighter way to bring everything. Only truly desperate backpackers will go as far as to remove the strings and tags from their teabags, but it does happen.

Finally, avoid campsite confusion, frustration, and possible mayhem along the lines of "So where is the spaghetti now that we've cooked the sauce?" Before you pack, divide all the food you're going to bring into piles, each representing a meal. Then bag each meal separately. Put the spaghetti with the spaghetti sauce, put the right amount of powdered milk with the pancake mix, and so forth. Some hikers suggest color coding the bags so that a breakfast bag, for example, is clearly not going to be mistaken for one containing lunch or dinner food. A fourth color bag can contain staples and condiments.

WATER, WATER

All this attention to food is not meant in any way to diminish the importance of water. You can live for weeks with no food, but with no water, you'll be in big trouble after only a few days. All of your meals and snacks should be accompanied by plentiful liquids.

The bare essentials: appropriate clothing, food, and gear.

QUEST FOR FIRE

These days, it's foolhardy to head off on any sort of camping trip expecting to do all your cooking on a campfire. In many places, wood is hard to come by, and in others—more and more—fires aren't permitted at all.

That's okay, actually, because camping stoves are no longer the technological dinosaurs many of us remember from camp. Most are small, lightweight, easy to use, and quite reliable. In fact, the biggest problem they seem to pose these days is how to choose among them.

If you're going to buy a stove, you've got to start by deciding what type of fuel you want to use. Each has its good points, but there are the negatives to consider as well.

If you're going to the ends of the earth, you're going to find kerosene widely available when you get there. And it probably won't cost you too much. But it does smoke, and a kerosene stove can be hard to light.

So a lot of people prefer butane, which, though harder to find, will burn instantly, cleanly, and relatively safely, in warm weather, at least. In cold weather, butane just vaporizes—it won't burn.

That's why the Europeans have been adding propane to the mixture for years. This blended fuel is a great convenience, but since it's just recently been introduced in the United States, it's not yet widely available. Straight propane, by the way, is not really suitable for backpacking, since it's stored in a heavy canister. (The lightweight butane canister is easy to carry, but when it's empty it's easy to leave behind. Don't. Always pack out your empty canisters, no matter how many you may find littering your campsites.)

Cooking camp-style.

White gas can be pretty easy to get your hands on, and it's not too expensive. But it is volatile. And gas stoves require priming, which can be a nuisance. This fuel, by the way, is a cleaner, additive-free version of the gas we use to fuel our cars.

Then there's denatured alcohol, whose main asset is its relative safety. Also, being a nonpetroleum-based product, it suits some campers' political and environmental agenda.

Some new stoves actually use good old-fashioned wood as a fuel. Many are surprisingly efficient, but they do kind of bring you back to the campfire problem: To fuel them, you must be at a place where you're allowed to gather wood and can actually find some.

Once you've decided what type of fuel will suit your needs—many people settle on butane for warm-weather cooking and white gas for more trying conditions—there are some questions you must now address about your prospective stove. How much does it weigh? How easy is it to set up and to light? Is the flame adjustable? Is it designed so that it will stay standing up, or is it easy to tip over? How long will it take to heat up a quart of water, and how efficiently does it use its fuel? Outdoor magazines often run features testing the latest stoves. Try to consult a recent issue before you buy.

Remember that cold weather and high altitude will have a pronounced effect on your stove. Be sure you understand what to expect and how to handle it before you go.

COOKING OVER A FIRE

If you happen to be at a campsite stocked with good firewood in a season when fires are actually permitted, the first thing many people will tell you to do is to go out and catch a trout.

Trout are wonderful grilled or pan-fried in butter, margarine, or oil. Or find a long, flexible green stick and thread it through the fish so you can roast it over the flames.

An alternate method is to season a fish and then wrap it in a few layers of foil and place the package directly on the coals. This method works equally well with potatoes and whole ears of corn.

In general, campfires are hot, hotter than you might expect, so keep a close eye on whatever you are cooking. And be careful—try not to lose half of it in the flames, as some of us are wont to do.

WHEN YOU COOK OVER A FIRE, THE OUTSIDE OF YOUR POTS WILL GET BLACK. SOME PEOPLE SAY THEY ALWAYS COAT THEIR POTS' BOTTOMS WITH A LAYER OF SOAP BEFORE USE SO THAT THE BLACK WILL WASH RIGHT OFF AFTERWARDS. OTHERS SAY THE BLACK GUNK HELPS DISTRIBUTE THE HEAT AND EVEN TOUT A COMMERCIAL BLACKENER TO AID IN THE PROCESS.

A camping stove can provide you with a hot cup of coffee or tea anytime of the day or night.

Cooking on the trail can be a real treat, especially when fresh trout is on the menu.

Pots and Pans and Other Utensils

The Sierra cup is a camping classic. And for good reason. It's a drinking cup, measuring cup, and bowl. The only thing better than a Sierra cup for hot drinks is an insulated cup.

Beginners usually buy pre-assembled cooksets, including a pot or two, a pot handle, a bowl, and a cup. But many experienced backpackers prefer to assemble their cookware piece by piece, including a small Teflon frying pan.

Don't forget a spatula, a small ladle, a spoon, and a knife. If your pocketknife doesn't have one, pack a can opener. And if you're planning to cook on a fire, don't forget a small folding grill.

No Cooking Necessary

Now, for the moment at least, forget all of the above. Let's say you're planning a backpacking trip, but you're not going to bring a stove and, no, you're not going to cook over an open fire, either. Think about it. Immediately your pack feels lighter, doesn't it? No stove, no fuel, no pots, no utensils.

If you're not going for very long or would just like to experiment, you'll find that you can do quite well on a no-cooking diet. Substitute lots of nuts, toasted grains, dried fruits, cheese, dried meat, and so on—whatever appeals to you—for your usual foods.

With no cooking to contend with—and no after-meal clean-up necessary—you'll find that you have more hours in the day. There's more time for exploring, reading, or just plain relaxing.

The merits of no-cooking camping are clearest in the summertime, when you won't be depending on a hot meal to warm you up. Be careful, though, and don't negate the emotional and physical value of a hot meal (especially in cold weather) when you're planning your trip.

One Last Thing

Pack a treat, and pack it deep down in the depths of your pack where you won't see it all the time. Then, when you can't stand one more meal of macaroni and cheese or one more taste of gorp, dig down and pull it out. Don't underestimate the pleasure a special tidbit can give, whether it's a box of Jordan almonds, a can of smoked oysters, a small bottle of brandy, or a tightly wrapped (and now completely thawed) package of frozen raspberries.

Chapter Six

Being careful, the first step to a safe backpacking trip.

Staying Healthy

Most of us spend most of our lives within easy reach of medical care. A few steps from the medicine cabinet, with its Band-Aids™, cough syrup, and aspirin; a phone call away from our doctor; a block or a five-minute drive from the nearest drugstore.

This ready access helps keep us healthy—but it can also make a trip into the wilderness seem like a terrifying leap into a world without help. We wonder: What happens if something goes wrong out there? How will I take care of myself?

We've all heard the horror stories; often, horror stories are all you hear about those who brave the backcountry. What we don't hear enough of are the

Follow the rules!

millions of people who backpack every year and return with glowing stories of the miles they covered or the scenery they saw, not about the legs they broke or the snakes that bit them.

There's no denying that health problems—including serious ones—do occur on the trail. Remember, though, that the most frequent threats to a backpacker's health—and to enjoyment of the trip—are such mundane problems as blisters, insect bites, and sunburn. With a little care, you can avoid (or at least minimize) these as well as the more serious problems.

By now you may be getting sick of hearing about the need for careful preparation—but it's still the best guarantee for a safe, uneventful hike. If you just throw some clothes into an old backpack and head out into the backcountry, you'll be courting disaster.

Follow these easy guidelines, though, and you'll be far less likely to get in trouble.

This chapter will give you a sense of the possible accidents, diseases, and other conditions that can occur on any trip. But it's no substitute for far more detailed knowledge available elsewhere. If you're planning a wilderness trip, take an outdoor survival course; your outdoor store should have information about where such courses are taught.

Even if you're just heading up the trail for a few days, please refer to "For Further Reading" on page 171 for a list of books containing important first-aid information. Then buy one and bring it along. You may never need it, but . . . .

E X E R C I S E , E X E R C I S E , E X E R C I S E

First of all, get in shape. Make sure your muscles are strong before you leave. Even well-groomed trails can be rough, bumpy, filled with unseen roots, rocks, and other hazards. Nothing will ruin a hike more quickly than a sprained ankle or twisted knee. If you do enough damage, you may find yourself having to be carried out. This is not a pleasant way to end a trip, for you or for the friends who have to do the carrying.

You can't expect a body that's spent years without exercise (regular walks to the corner doughnut shop don't count) to transform itself into a lean machine the moment you hit the trail. Regular exercise will strengthen your muscles, which in turn will help protect your joints. The result: You'll be far less likely to suffer an injury from a misstep or fall. You'll also help avoid overuse injuries—often the bane of unprepared hikers' existence.

For details on the best way to exercise yourself to a happier hike, see Chapter 1 and delve into the wide variety of books and videos available in every bookstore and library.

CARRY THE RIGHT STUFF

Wear jeans, and you're risking hypothermia. Hike the Continental Divide Trail in cheap sneakers, and your feet will be a mass of blisters by the second day. Pay no attention to the weather conditions that may occur during your trip, and you may find yourself trying to reach your hiking destination in wind, rain, or snow. Normally, these would be an annoyance to be waited out. Your lack of preparation, however, would transform them into life-threatening emergencies—or at least guarantee that you'll be honking and snorting with the worst cold of your life for the rest of the trip.

The most important key to avoiding serious problems on the trail is to know what you're getting into. Read up about your route. Don't assume that the warm, calm weather prevailing now is likely to continue. Find out the worst conditions that may occur, and assume that they will plague you throughout your trip. (Yes, this sounds like a depressing way to prepare for a trip, but think of how happy you'll be when you're blessed with ideal conditions instead.)

Then bring the right clothes, the right gear—everything you might possibly, even unexpectedly, need.

FIRST AID: THE KIT'S THE THING

Even if you pack your portable phone with you on your through-hike of the Appalachian Trail, you might have trouble getting a drug store to deliver.

So you'd better bring along whatever medicines, bandages, and other health aids you may possibly need. The only completely dependable first-aid kit is one that's been planned and put together well before departure date.

First, of course, make sure you pack any special medications you may need. You can never be over-prepared. If you suffer from some chronic condition, carry the treatment—even if you haven't had any trouble for months. There's nothing like being hundreds of miles from the nearest pharmacy or telephone to cause a flare-up.

Next, it's essential to plan for the bumps and bruises that may occur on almost any hike. Blisters, skin infections, slightly pulled muscles—none are life-

Far from the nearest hospital.

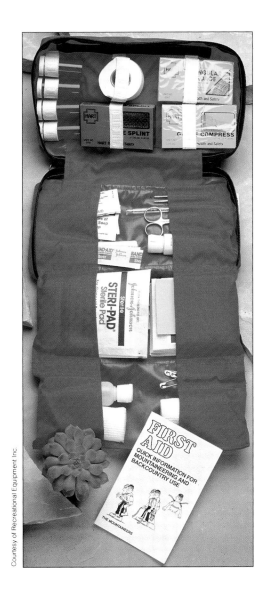

Courtesy of Recreational Equipment Inc

You can buy a premade first-aid kit or make one yourself.

threatening, but all are a sure ticket to a miserable experience, if you don't have the means to treat them. Even an unexpected head cold (a frequent occurrence, as your body may have trouble adjusting to wind, rain, or unexpectedly cold weather) can plague you for days, if you're not prepared.

Every wilderness expert, every outdoor magazine, every hiker's manual has its own "perfect" first-aid kit. Provided here is our list of first-aid necessities, complete with comments and explanations, that gives you a base to build on. The numbers are only suggestions; of course, you won't need as much if you're just going on an overnight, and you may want to bring even more if you're planning a long trek over rough terrain. No one will think any less of you if you toss in a few extra aspirin.

THE BASIC KIT

- 12 plastic strips (Band-Aids™ or other brand)
- 1 roll cloth adhesive tape, one to two inches in diameter
- 10 sterile gauze pads, three inches by three inches
- 1 larger sterile gauze pad, eight inches by eight inches or thereabouts
- 1 roll sterile gauze, three inches wide (the gauze pads are designed for abrasions and other injuries, while this roll can be used for compresses)
- 1 tube antibiotic ointment or cream (essential for preventing burns from becoming infected and for keeping small infections from blossoming)
- 12 broad-spectrum antibiotic tablets (if you're unlucky enough to contract pneumonia or some other general infection, you must have something to fight it. See your doctor for the best choice for you)
- 20 headache tablets (aspirin and ibuprofen, if you can tolerate them, also help reduce inflammation)
- Tylenol with codeine (when aspirin isn't enough—for example, if you have a severely sprained ankle or other joint injury—this will help you hike out)
- 20 decongestant or antihistamine/decongestant tablets (necessary if you're allergy-prone. If you've got a head cold, they may enable you to enjoy the days on the trail more, and ward off a more serious illness by sleeping better at night)
- Moleskin, Spenco Second Skin, and other products to help prevent blisters and to treat them once they appear
- 4 needles (even a splinter can cause untold misery, if you can't dig it out)
- scissors

With a few personal variations, this kit should enable you to cope with most threats for full enjoyment of your trip. But you may feel you need even greater protection. The following alphabetical list of common injuries and other potential trek-wreckers—and how best to deal with them—should provide some additional clues. Use your own judgment, but remember: If you've got room in your pack, six ounces of extra medicine may save you tons of trouble.

BEE STINGS

For most of us, a bee sting is just an annoyance. It hurts and raises a lump that itches for a few days. If that seems unacceptable, bring along one of the many over-the-counter lotions that reduce the effects of stings.

For some people, however, a bee sting can be far more serious. It can even be fatal. These people suffer intense allergic reactions that can cause hives, rapid heartbeat, inflammation of the throat that can interfere with breathing, and even rapid death from shock.

If you're allergic to bee stings, talk to your doctor before taking any hike. He or she will prescribe a kit containing a needle and syringe and a vial of epinephrine, a chemical that counteracts the effects of this and other severe allergic reactions. Be sure to read all instructions on the shock-prevention kit *before* your hike. You may even want to get hold of an extra syringe, fill it with water, and practice giving shots (on an orange or a grapefruit) until you're comfortable with the practice.

Resting tired muscles.

BLISTERS

By far the most frequent destroyer of hiking plans is the lowly blister. So it's the injury that any hiker should take the most care to prevent and treat.

There are two types of blisters: The ones that break and the ones that don't. If you have to have a blister, the latter are far preferable, so the moment you feel any discomfort, inspect the area. A reddened area—a "hot spot"—will soon become a blister if left untended.

If you've got a hot spot or an unburst blister, try to keep it that way. Isolate it from the area of the shoe that's caused it by covering it with moleskin. This should allow the blister to subside over time.

If the blister breaks, treat it as you would a small burn. Take great pains to avoid infection. Again, it's important to pad the wound and keep it from being further abraded.

BURNS

It's the first night of your weeklong backpack, and you're relaxing comfortably in front of the fire with your boots off, listening to the various sounds of the wilderness. You reach out to adjust a log, and only then discover that you're holding a red-hot end. You've got a burn.

Clean the wound with the purest water you've got, cover it with antibiotic ointment, and protect it with a gauze pad. Then keep an eye on it. If it becomes infected, you may want to start a course of oral antibiotic tablets.

If a more serious burn occurs, seek medical help as soon as possible.

GIARDIASIS

It's been a long day, and you're thirsty. You round a bend in the trail, and there's the cold, clear, rushing stream you've been hearing for the past half hour. You want nothing more than to bend over and drink great draughts of this sparkling mountain ambrosia.

The culprit, as every experienced hiker knows, is a tiny protozoan called giardia. Transmitted, usually in the form of a miniscule cyst, by means of feces (human, beaver, deer, and probably livestock as well), giardia flourishes in fresh water—and also in the human intestine, where it becomes a disease called giardiasis.

The first symptoms of the disease will not surface for one to two weeks after you're infected, when you'll begin to suffer from severe diarrhea, cramps, bloating, gas, and sometimes vomiting. You won't be able to keep anything you eat or drink down, so your weight will plummet. In the backcountry, this condition can be fatal. Left untreated, giardiasis can become a chronic, debilitating condition. Know the symptoms of giardiasis, mentioned above, and if there is any doubt in your mind, see a doctor *immediately.*

While various water-purification systems—iodine tablets or crystals, chlorine-liberating tablets, and various filters have been touted for their ability to eliminate giardia and other organisms, the best solution is still boiling all water. Boil it for at least twenty minutes.

HEAT EXHAUSTION AND HEAT STROKE

Even the most experienced backpackers aren't supermen and superwomen— but many think they are. The result can be severe problems caused by

© Jeff Foott

Stay healthy: Purify your water.

© Doug Sokell/Tom Stack & Associates

overheating, which causes the body to lose crucial fluids and salt, resulting in a decrease of the blood supply to the brain.

The lesser—but still serious—problem, is heat exhaustion, characterized by headaches, dizziness, and weakness. It's essential that anyone showing these symptoms be taken to a cool, shady place (if possible). The victim should then loosen or remove her clothes and lie down; her companions should fan her, sponge her with water, and give her sips of cool water to drink.

If left unattended, heat exhaustion can become heat stroke. In addition to headache and weakness, the victim will have fever, flushed skin, nausea and vomiting, a rapid, pounding pulse, and—a sure sign—she will *not* be sweating.

This condition can be fatal. The victim must be undressed, sponged with cool water, given aspirin or acetaminophen and cool water to drink. Take the victim to a doctor as soon as possible.

Heat problems can be avoided with a little care. Drink lots of water all day long, keep your salt level up by snacking frequently, wear a hat in hot, sunny areas, and rest if you feel yourself being affected by the heat. You might not reach your destination as quickly, but you'll arrive there in much better shape.

Under the hot desert sun: Bryce Canyon, Utah.

HYPOTHERMIA

One of the greatest threats to backpackers, hypothermia (which occurs when the body's temperature falls about three degrees below the normal 98.6 degrees F) is, if not treated, an extremely serious condition, and can be fatal. Yet it doesn't only strike backpackers in the Arctic or on snowy mountaintops—it can also occur in moderate climes. You can die from hypothermia as easily in Oregon in April as in Wyoming in January, unless you understand the symptoms and treatments.

Heat loss leading to hypothermia can be brought on by one or more of the following conditions: exhaustion, wetness (caused by rain, snow, or even sweat), wind, or cold weather. With remarkable speed and severity, these conditions begin the process, as the body, trying to fend off the encroaching cold, attempts to keep the heart and other internal organs warm. As a result, the extremities will grow colder, and blood flow to the brain will be impeded. This produces the most serious symptoms of hypothermia.

Climbing on Cotopaxi, Ecuador.

These symptoms include violent shivering followed by no shivering at all, slurred speech, difficulty in walking, loss of muscular control, overwhelming drowsiness, and irrationality. If your companion has some of these symptoms, he must be treated—even if he irrationally insists that he's fine.

Treatment must be undertaken immediately; untreated victims of hypothermia can die in under two hours. Follow these steps:

• Find or make shelter from the wind or rain.

• Replace the victim's clothing with warm, dry clothing.

• Warm the victim with moderate heat. Use a fire if possible. If not, wrap the victim in a sleeping bag and climb in with him; your body heat may keep him alive. Remember to insulate both of you (or all of you) from the cold ground.

• Keep the victim awake.

• If possible, give him warm water or soup to drink. *Do not* administer alcohol, coffee, or tea.

• Above all, treat the victim gently. His system in this condition is very fragile, and sudden movements or shocks can even cause a heart attack.

• Once the victim has warmed up again, allow him to rest for a while. Then get him to a hospital.

Once again, the best way to treat hypothermia is to avoid it. Know the temperature and other weather conditions that *may* occur (not only those that are likely), follow the rules of layering, and protect yourself from even the slightest possibility of this deadly condition.

Mosquito and Other Insect Bites

(Note: For a discussion of tick bites—a very different problem—see page 71.)

Walk unprotected through a swarm of black flies or a swamp filled with mosquitoes, and you soon discover another threat to the success of your trip: bug bites.

You can't prevent them entirely—but unless you're planning a trip in an insect-free zone, you'd better try. Dress properly—in long pants, a long-sleeved shirt, and maybe even a head net. Most people also bring along a lotion or spray containing the chemical DEET. While conventional wisdom says that you should use a formulation that is 90 percent DEET or more, some recent studies indicate that long-lasting products with 35 percent DEET may work just as well, or even better.

© Christopher C. Bain

Shelter in the snow.

Unfortunately, DEET is very oily, smells bad, and can damage rayon, spandex, and other materials. It can even cause irritability and other side effects, particularly in children. Therefore, it may be wise to stick with formulations containing lower concentrations of DEET, and use them sparingly.

Or try one of the alternative products: Avon Skin-So-Soft (a bath oil that some people swear by, and others at); eucalyptus oil; or even a sonic mosquito repeller, which imitates the wingbeat frequency of a dragonfly, the mosquito's mortal enemy.

MOUNTAIN SICKNESS

This condition encompasses a variety of symptoms that usually begin occurring after the hiker attains altitudes of ten thousand feet or higher, especially in people who have over-exerted or are dehydrated. These symptoms, which can include persistent headache, nausea, vomiting, and difficulty breathing, result from the body's inability to adjust to rapid increases in altitude.

In mild cases, aspirin will control the headache, and spending a day or two without climbing any higher will give your body time to acclimatize. In more severe cases—or if symptoms don't disappear soon—it's advisable to descend one or two thousand feet, then wait.

Important note: Any time you're planning a trek that involves high-altitude hiking, be sure to take a course or at least read a book beforehand that describes possible symptoms of—and treatments for—mountain sickness.

POISON OAK, IVY, AND SUMAC

Hiker beware: poison ivy.

If you learn to recognize these plants and then don't touch them, you'll be safer on the trail.

But if you have mistakenly hiked through a patch of any of these plants, you're likely to be in for a bad time. In milder cases, within two days of exposure you'll begin to suffer from a rapidly spreading, itchy, blistering rash. People who are more sensitive may end up in the hospital.

Unfortunately, there's no immediate cure for poison oak, ivy, or sumac. If you realize you've been exposed, wash the affected area or areas with cold, soapy water as soon as possible (although some experts say only detergent or heavy-duty soap are effective here). Once the rash begins, regular application of hydrocortisone cream can control the worst symptoms.

S NAKEBITE

First: Know your snakes. Very few are poisonous.

If you're in an area with no poisonous snakes and you get bitten, the worst you'll suffer is an infection, which can be treated with antibiotics. But if an unknown, possibly poisonous snake has just sunk its fangs into your leg, then you should be prepared.

If the snake was poisonous, you'll know soon enough. You'll get a bad taste or a tingling sensation in your mouth. Within an hour, the area around the bite will become swollen and painful. You may then begin to feel dizzy, feverish, headachy, and lightheaded.

If at all possible, get yourself to a hospital. If you're within an hour or two of a road, walk out as quickly as you can, getting anyone to help you. Don't forget to rest periodically, and don't drink any alcohol.

If you're deep in the backcountry, this may not be possible. In these cases, the foresight that you showed in bringing a snakebite kit will be rewarded. These kits, which contain a sharp blade, constrictive band, and suction cups, will allow you to suck at least some of the venom out of the wound. *Follow all instructions on the kit exactly,* then seek help as soon as possible.

AN OUTLANDISH NEW METHOD OF COUN-TERACTING SNAKEBITES HAS RECENTLY RE-CEIVED A LOT OF PUBLICITY. IT INVOLVES ADMINISTRATION OF A STRONG, HIGH-VOLTAGE, LOW-AMPERAGE ELECTRIC SHOCK TO THE WOUND AND NEARBY AREAS. ITS PROPONENTS RECOMMEND USING A STUN GUN OF THE SORT USED BY POLICE OFFICERS.

THIS METHOD HAS BEEN IN THE FOLK-LORE FOR YEARS, AND IT MAY, IN FACT, WORK. BUT ITS EFFECTIVENESS HAS NEVER BEEN PROVEN, AND MOST DOCTORS ARE SKEPTICAL. BUYER BEWARE.

S UNBURN

Sunburns seem like a pretty mundane worry, something to be more careful about during a day on a beach than in the midst of a month-long trek. But sunburns can happen anywhere—and have you ever tried to carry a heavy backpack on badly burned shoulders?

A sunburn can cause a variety of problems above and beyond simple discomfort. Bad burns can cause blistering—you might as well have exposed the back of your neck to your campfire. In addition, people with sunburn can suffer from fever, chills, and other flulike symptoms.

Although you can treat sunburn as you would other burns and infections, why not simply prevent them? Sunscreen lotions are available everywhere, with sun-protection factors (SPFs) ranging from three to thirty-six and beyond. Bring the one that's best for you and the terrain you'll be covering, and use it!

T ICK BITES

Most of us grew up knowing about ticks—those creatures that infested our pets during the summer months, and sometimes got hold of us, too.

Though dog ticks occasionally transmit disease to humans, they're virtually harmless when compared to the tiny deer tick. Now found in nearly every state, and increasing in numbers everywhere, this is the dreaded purveyor of Lyme disease—one of the backpacker's worst enemies.

The deer tick ranges from the size of a poppyseed to perhaps a third the size of a dog tick. It inhabits weed-infested fields and other off-trail environments, and is particularly abundant where deer are common (though it also shows up in areas where deer are virtually absent). The bite causes no pain; you're likely never to know you've been bitten until you start feeling the symptoms of Lyme disease.

These symptoms frequently begin with a dark rash (often in a bull's-eye shape around the bite site), days or weeks after the bite occurred. Later, the victim may feel flulike symptoms that last for several days, followed later by intense arthritic symptoms in the knees and other joints; heart irregularities; and even memory loss and other central nervous system complications.

When diagnosed early, Lyme disease can be easily treated with antibiotics. Still, the best way to treat it is to avoid it—a great challenge, admittedly, if you're in the midst of a cross-country hike. If you're in a heavily infested area, try to avoid fields with high weeds, and always tuck your pants into your boots if you're going off the trail. In addition, apply a bug repellent containing DEET to socks, cuffs, and other areas where ticks may hitch a ride.

You may also want to bring along Permanone, an aerosol spray containing permethrin, a guaranteed tick killer. *Use it only on your clothes, and never apply it directly on your skin.*

IMPORTANT: Using a magnifying glass, always check yourself carefully for ticks at the end of each day; attached ticks need hours (and sometimes days) to transmit Lyme disease. If you find an attached tick, take a pair of tweezers, grasp the tick behind its head, and pull it carefully out. If you can, keep the tick in a small bottle or vial, so you can take it to a doctor and have it tested for the bacteria that cause Lyme disease.

If you have an attached tick, don't automatically cancel the rest of your trip. An extra few days between bite and diagnosis won't make much difference, but you must see a doctor when you return home. If you're in the midst of a months-long trek, however, and either find a tick or start feeling some of the symptoms mentioned above, don't waste any time. Get yourself to a doctor. The disease is easy to treat in its early stages, but harder later on.

© Sharon Gerig/Tom Stack & Associates

A solo hiker takes the shady trail to Marcy Dam near Lake Placid in Adirondack Park, New York.

Hiking the old-growth, Tongass National Forest, Alaska.

HIT THE TRAIL

Finally, after all this planning, here you are on the trail, a backpack on your back. You've studied a variety of maps, so you know exactly where you're going. All you have to do is go up this hill, around this bend, over this stream, and turn right on the intersecting trail, which will take you to the shelter where you'll spend the night. But you've gone up the hill, round the bend, and over the stream, and—no matter how hard you look—there is no intersecting trail to be found.

So you plod on, sticking to the main trail, which by now has turned left and is heading resolutely in the wrong direction. Eventually, a mile or two later, you do come to another trail, and you decide to take it. It's a lovely walk, with all

ALWAYS MAKE SURE YOU HAVE A PENCIL AND PAPER WITH YOU. THAT WAY YOU'LL BE AVAILABLE TO RECORD YOUR REVELATIONS AS THEY HAPPEN, BUT—MORE CRITICALLY—YOU'LL BE ABLE TO MAKE CORRECTIONS AND ADDITIONS ON YOUR MAP. YOU'LL ALSO FIND IT HANDY TO JOT DOWN IDEAS OF THINGS TO PACK AND THINGS TO FORGET TO PACK WHEN YOU'RE PREPARING FOR YOUR NEXT TRIP.

© Christopher C. Bain

Plotting a course.

sorts of twists and turns and beautiful scenery to look at. But then gradually the trail fades away, and before you know it, you're lost. Lost in a park with a well-marked trail system and two good maps in your pocket.

USING A COMPASS AND A MAP

That's why—even if you're not even thinking about heading off into the untracked wilderness—you've got to have some basic navigation skills. These skills can save your trip and enhance the whole experience. With basic map-reading abilities, you'll notice alternate routes and water sources and old mines and fishing ponds and all manner of other treasures that you wouldn't even imagine if you simply stayed with your eyes glued to the trail.

You don't have to be a first-class orienteer to be able to cope, but do learn how to use a map and compass. The best place to do this is at home, well in advance of your trip. There are a couple of good books on the subject. Get one and read it (see pages 171-172 for suggestions).

By itself, a compass is of limited use, especially for a beginner. Sure, it'll tell you north from south and east from west, and that might even be enough to help you find your way. But it's in conjunction with a good topographical map that a compass really comes into its own. First learn to read a topo map. A good way to help those abstract squiggles take on a sense of real meaning is to take a map of an area you know along on a hike. Before you start, locate your position and a couple of other familiar landmarks. Compare the squiggles on the map with the real thing. Continue doing this as you walk. Notice how the lines of a steep hill tell a story, as do the indications of a flat stretch. Notice how streams, swamps, and other landmarks are indicated.

As your map-reading skills improve, you'll know what to expect in a place you've never been to before, just by studying the map. You'll be able to plan an itinerary with the knowledge that certain stretches of trail are flat and others impossibly hilly.

Then you'll be ready to use that powerful navigational tool, a map and compass together. All you have to do is line up north on your map with north on your compass and allow for declination (the difference between true north and magnetic north). If you know where you are, you'll be able to identify surrounding landmarks. And if you've lost your way but are able to spot a couple of landmarks, you'll be able to figure out where you are. A fairly accurate sense of direction will help you find your way.

OTHER WAYS TO NAVIGATE

You don't need a compass to tell due north. Simply noticing the location of the sunrise or sunset ought to be able to get you at least generally oriented. But generally isn't always good enough.

That's the problem with a lot of old fabled ways of telling direction. You often hear that you can use your wristwatch to find south, assuming it's sunny out. First, it is said that you should turn the watch so that the hour hand (don't forget to adjust it for Standard Time, if necessary) points to the sun. Due south is supposed to be located halfway between the hour hand and the number 12. In fact, this is only a very rough way to tell direction, but it might help if you're in a real bind.

Another tip you hear is that you can plant a stick vertically in the ground and make a mark at the end of its shadow. Wait fifteen minutes, and mark the end of the new shadow. Connect the dots, and you've got a line going east-west, with the first point to the west. But, according to the Sierra Club's *Land Navigation Handbook,* this method is accurate to within only 20 or 30 degrees, which is to say that it's not very accurate at all.

Some hikers like to use a pedometer so that they will know the distance they've traveled, down to the last foot. Pedometers can help with navigation, too—if you can spot your starting place on a map, and you know how far you've walked, you can zero in on your likely location. Or at least you can rule out the impossible ones.

If you like gadgets, you might consider acquiring an altimeter. With it, you can tell your vertical position, which can help you find your position on a map. If you're climbing a long hill, it'll help you judge how much farther you have to go. These lightweight, handy devices work best if they are kept at a constant temperature; don't carry an altimeter close to your body where it's nice and warm and then expect it to perform accurately when suddenly exposed to cold mountain air. Hang it around your neck on the outside of your clothing or keep it tucked in your pack.

WHAT TO DO IF YOU'RE LOST

First of all, don't panic.

Keep a positive attitude: Remember that with all your planning and thinking and anticipating, you'll be able to get out of this. The vast majority of such situations are easily resolved.

LEARN A LITTLE BASIC STAR IDENTIFICATION TO HELP YOU NAVIGATE BY THE STARS. CONNECT THE TWO STARS ON THE OUTER EDGE OF THE BIG DIPPER'S DIPPER, AND CONTINUE THAT LINE FOR ABOUT FIVE TIMES THE DISTANCE BETWEEN THE STARS, AND YOU'LL FIND THE NORTH STAR.

© Tom Stack & Associates

Don't depend on the stars, unless you know what you're doing.

IF YOU'RE LOST AND WANT TO GET OUT, GO DOWNHILL. PEOPLE LIVE IN VALLEYS, AND ROADS GO THROUGH THEM AS WELL. ALSO, YOU'LL FIND WATER IN VALLEYS.

Staying the course in Manning Park, British Columbia.

Sit down, conserve your energy, and go over what's happened. Pull out your maps and try to retrace your steps, using visible landmarks to help identify your location. If it's still light out, try a couple of scouting expeditions, but be very cautious not to go around in exhausting circles. If night is falling and you have your pack containing food, water, clothing, and shelter, try to look at it this way: You're not really lost—you're about to camp in a new campsite. Settle in and have a good meal and a good rest, and save the route finding for the next day.

If you don't have your gear with you, then your main concern should be staying warm. Find or create some sort of shelter for yourself, especially if it's cold or rainy out. Build a fire and keep it going. The smoke will attract people who may be looking for you. If your clothes are wet, take them off and dry them over the fire. Think of ways to make it easy for anyone who's looking for you to find your position. If you have a whistle with you, blow it repeatedly, and if you have a mirror or other shiny object, try flashing it during daylight. Take short walks to try to find the trail, but be sure that you can find your way back to your campsite before dark. Remember, never leave your shelter at night, when it's easy to get even more lost than you already are.

There is not enough room in this book to detail other survival techniques, but many books on the subject exist. It's a good idea to read one and familiarize yourself with various recommended techniques, especially if you're doing some winter or high-altitude camping or are heading out to a particularly rugged and unpopulated area.

HOME SWEET CAMP

A vast majority of the time, getting lost is simply a momentary affair—brought on by missing the turn onto the trail you were looking for or by finding that the map and the topography disagree.

After such an adventure—or any of the more benign sort involved in a day of hiking—there's a lot of pleasure to be gleaned from the rituals of setting up camp and making yourself at home.

There's little to say about camping at a shelter or a developed campsite. Sometimes there will be other people there; sometimes you'll be by yourself. Sometimes the other people will be more sociable than you; sometimes less. It's really very simple: If everyone has a reasonable amount of respect for each other, things usually work out fine.

But camping in the backcountry, or just off the beaten path, requires a little more thought. Let's pause for a moment to consider exactly what we are about to do. We are about to invade an area that doesn't belong to us—or even to our species. We must show it—and the other species—appropriate respect. We must try to fit in inconspicuously, so that other hikers in the area won't even know we're there. We must leave behind no permanent mark of our stay.

In these days when parklands are vanishing at every turn, and when even the most pristine wilderness areas are victims of pollution, we must be especially careful to preserve the wilderness we still have.

Choosing a campsite, therefore, is an exercise in common sense and sensitivity. You want to find a surface that can support a certain amount of traffic but that will be at least moderately comfortable to sleep on. Sand and gravel do very well, as does a clearing in forest. Just be careful to avoid trampling fragile vegetation.

You want to be near a source of water, but you don't want it to be running right through the site. Be careful about selecting a dry riverbed as your campsite—it'll be dry and comfortable, as long as there's no flash flood.

Avoid game trails, or you'll find that you'll have some visitors you probably won't want, and look out for "widow makers," those standing dead trees that can blow over in a puff of wind.

YOU CAN ESTIMATE THE AMOUNT OF TIME UNTIL SUNSET BY EXTENDING YOUR ARM IN FRONT OF YOU TOWARD THE SUN WITH YOUR WRIST BENT IN, FINGERS TOGETHER JUST BELOW THE SUN. COUNT THE NUMBER OF FINGER WIDTHS BETWEEN THE SUN AND THE HORIZON. EACH FINGER IS WORTH APPROXIMATELY FIFTEEN MINUTES.

© Spencer Swanger/Tom Stack & Associates

Elk Mountains, Colorado.

© Bob Winsett/Tom Stack & Associates

Making camp.

Pitch your tent on high ground to avoid flooding, and forget the old habit of digging a ditch around the tent's perimeter.

Set up your cooking area nearby. If there is plenty of deadwood available, and there's no rule against it, build a fire. But keep it small, away from overhanging branches and roots. Make your fire in a pit (purists retain the top layer of sod, water it religiously, and replace it when they leave), not a ring. Collect only as much wood as you absolutely need, and burn it all completely. Don't leave a half-burned log to mark your passing.

Many times these days, people decide not to bother with fires, or they aren't permitted anyway. Cooking with a stove reduces one's impact to the minimum. It doesn't lend the same mood (people rarely gather to tell stories or sing songs around the stove), but it does have the bonuses of being quick and easy.

A FLUID SITUATION

Camp near, but not too near, a source of water. Remember that the local animals need water, too, so keep your distance, especially if there's not much water around.

These days, there's really no such thing as water that's safe to drink, even in the wilderness. Boil all drinking water, for at least twenty minutes, *always*. Don't rely on a filter or purifying tablets unless you have no option—they simply don't do as good a job.

If you're going to bathe, do everything you can to avoid getting soap (even biodegradable soap) in the water. Use the water at the source just for getting wet, and carry water away for rinsing.

The same goes for dishwashing. If you must use soap, use it a distance away from the water source. But note that most environment-conscious people no longer wash dishes and pots with soap or detergent. They find that sand, pine needles, or gravel can scrub away anything a soapy sponge can handle, and a boiling water rinse takes care of the rest.

That rinse is an element of basic camping hygiene that many people tend to take too lightly. The rule is to play it safe, every single thing that could eventually make contact with your digestive tract should be in contact only with treated water—so if you don't boil your washing water, be sure you rinse with boiling water. A rinse in iodized water, which will leave a disinfectant residue, is even safer.

THE BATHROOM

If there's an official outhouse nearby, use it. It's there for a reason.

But otherwise, you'll have to dig your own latrine. Choose your site carefully. It must be far away from a water source, and it must be in ground soft enough to dig in. Then, dig—almost a foot down. (Make sure you've packed a lightweight shovel for this purpose. If you're with a group, decide where the john is and place the shovel nearby. Anyone heading for the john will find it convenient to take—and use—the shovel, and anyone not finding the shovel in its appointed place will know to wait his or her turn.) Cover everything with plenty of dirt. And when you are ready to hike out, make sure you leave the area the way it looked when you got there.

Think twice about using toilet paper. Unless you're going to burn it up, you'd better be willing to pack it out. (Bring a plastic bag exclusively for that purpose.) Simply burying toilet paper isn't good enough. Animals will find it, dig it up, and decorate your campsite with it. Substitutes include leaves, soft pine needles, or a washable bandanna or other cloth, not so sanitary, but a lot better for the environment.

Even in the wilderness, there's no such thing as safe water to drink. Always boil for at least twenty minutes, *always.*

© Ron Spomer/Visuals Unlimited

Don't feed the bears!

NIGHT VISITORS

No matter how much cooking a hot meal over a hot campstove may resemble cooking over your gas range at home, you won't confuse the way to store your food at the campsite with just stashing everything in the fridge.

If you're staying at a popular campsite, you can be sure that it has its resident mice, chipmunks, squirrels, and raccoons—not to mention nearby bears and coyotes—who are well acquainted with the delicious morsels campers tend to have at hand. Sure, one of the pleasures of eating and sleeping outside is to join the animals in their habitat. But it's one thing to offer some nuts to a squirrel; it's a totally different thing to wake up at night to find that a family of mice—not to mention a bear—has moved in and taken judicious tastes of all your supplies before settling down to devour the most luscious goodies.

IN BEAR COUNTRY

If you're camping in grizzly territory, do your research. Find out if bears have been spotted in the area you're heading into, and make sure you pay close attention to the instructions on how to stash your food and what to do if you see a bear.

Despite the horror stories of teeth-gnashing fury, wild grizzlies will usually steer clear of any human contact. Despite their reputation, they're extremely shy animals. But some of them—particularly in some of the more well-visited national parks—have learned that humans tend to have food with them, and they like the food, so they won't always avoid contact. Sometimes they even seek it out.

Therefore, you have to take great pains to separate your food—and any smell of it—from yourself before you go to sleep. Hang your cooking gear and food in an approved bear-proof fashion, along with the clothes you wore to cook in. That way, if the bear wants the food, it won't have to go past you to reach it.

If you're hiking in grizzly land, do your absolute best to avoid any contact with the animals. Always be aware of your surroundings. Look for bear signs on the trail. Be aware of the wind direction and try to stay downwind of an area where you suspect a grizzly may be. If you spot one—and it doesn't see you—back off. Yes, you simply leave, and count yourself exceedingly lucky for having had the view.

But if the bear has seen you, and it doesn't just run off—which they'll do 90 percent of the time—then things are different. Try to back off slowly. Try to avoid contact.

But if that doesn't work, and the bear charges, then you're going to have to be brave and stand your ground—don't run; that would trigger the grizzly's instinct to chase you down. Imagine having to stand there while a 1,500-pound eight-foot long animal comes rushing at you full speed ahead. Experts say most charges are bluffs, but still, need we emphasize how hard you should work to avoid finding out for yourself?

When hiking in bear country, some people feel that making a certain amount of noise—singing, loud talking, attaching jingling "bear bells" to their packs or sticks—will warn the bears of your presence and allow them to move off. The idea is not to startle the bear—but to let it sense your presence first, to let it handle the situation its way, which means, usually, that it will run off.

Note that black bears, much smaller and less threatening than grizzlies, tend to be quite shy, though in many places—the southern part of the Appalachian Trail, for example—they have become extremely habituated to human company and human food and have become rather aggressive (and unnervingly insistent) beggars. The best way to avoid contact with them and other

Ignore at your own risk.

campsite pests is to pack your food carefully away in places or containers that the animals can't reach. Don't leave crumbs or leftovers around the campsite—finish off what you cook.

At Camp

Once you've set up camp, and you're through hiking until tomorrow, you are about to begin the part of the day that, for some people, makes all the hard work worthwhile. This is the time to pull out your paperback book and relax. To write in your journal. To take your camera on a short hike to explore and record your discoveries. To continue a long letter you never have time to write at home. To examine your maps and think about tomorrow's hike. To pull out your binoculars and a field guide and try to learn a little something about your surroundings. To look at the clouds and try to forecast tomorrow's weather. To simply kick back and relax and savor the very fact that you're out there.

For other people, these hours are just plain boring, and they'll complain. These are the people who can turn an enjoyable evening at camp into an impossible one. If they can't be convinced to lighten up, they should never be permitted to accompany you on the trails again.

Breaking Camp

The basic philosophy of minimum-impact camping dictates that before you take back to the trail, you must return the campsite to the untouched way it looked before you moved in.

If you had a fire, soak the ashes well, checking and double-checking for any remaining hot coals, scatter the ashes, and fill in the hole. Camouflage the area with loose grasses, leaves, and pine cones. Purists will also replace the sod that they retained (and watered). Fill in your latrine hole, and cover it over just as carefully.

Replace any rocks or logs that you may have moved, and try to restore any areas that show wear from your heavy pack, tent, or feet. You may also want to scatter unburned logs or kindling.

Once you're all packed up and ready to go, check the site one last time, looking for scraps of paper or material or anything else that might have been left behind.

In short: A hiker coming across this site even the very same day should spot no clues that you were there.

This camper on the High Divide in Olympia National Park, Washington, enjoys a spectacular, cloudless day.

© J. Lotter/Tom Stack & Associates

Chapter Eight

Togetherness in Olympic National Park, Washington.

The Backpacking Experience

Many years ago, the typical backpackers you'd see would be a small group of hardy young men. These days, men still hike with men, but now women hike with women, couples hike with couples, solo hikers are accompanied by their dogs, and families hit the trail en masse.

Each combination offers its own possibilities for pleasure—and also its own challenges. But, like everything else involved in hiking and camping, if you've thought about what might happen and prepare yourself in advance, you're likely to do just fine. More than just fine, actually—hiking and camping with different companions in various groups can make for a spectrum of entirely worthwhile and pleasurable experiences.

Always bring a baby carrier, which will turn your baby into an instant hiking companion.

Once the kids are big enough, they can hit the trail with you.

FAMILY AFFAIR

Camping vacations can be a wonderful opportunity for family fun. The key to successful camping *en famille* is planning, pure and simple. Make sure you bring the right things (and enough of them) to keep your kids dry, rested, well-fed, warm, safe, and entertained. And make sure you've thought about the special needs of each age group. Temper your own desires and habits with the knowledge of your kids' abilities and interests, and chances are you'll have a rewarding experience.

After becoming parents, many former staunch if-I-can't-carry-it-on-my-back-it's-not-coming backpackers suddenly discover the wonders of car camping. If you can drive to your campsite, you don't have to be concerned about carrying your baby, your baby's gear, and your own as well. It won't matter how much stuff you have to bring. You can spread out, sit back, and enjoy. And if you're enjoying it, chances are your child will too.

Some special concerns are:

Infants: Where will the baby sleep? A portable folding bed can come in handy. Where can he or she be placed safely during the day? Bring a seat—some car seats are perfect for this. Don't forget a baby carrier, which will turn your porta-baby into an instant hiking companion. Make sure you bring a mosquito net and insect repellent to put on the baby's clothes. (Check with your pediatrician for a repellent safe for a baby's skin.) Also be sure to keep the kid out of the sun, and see if your pediatrician can recommend a good sunscreen for infants. Plan your diaper strategy in advance, remembering the outdoor ethic: If you bring it in, pack it out.

Toddlers: The first thing for parents of toddlers to think about is safety. At camp, hazards abound (fuel, running water, fire, rocks, knives, etc.), and the trail offers its own set of perils. Some experienced hiking parents make sure young children always wear a bell, so that if they wander off, they'll be easily found; another recommendation is a name tag that includes medical information and also directions as to where you can be found.

Kids this age can begin to do a little hiking—but don't push them. Let them do as much as they enjoy. When their strength and sense of balance improve, they'll want to do even more.

A portable crib or playpen will come in handy at nighttime and naptime. Sleep, by the way, is a commodity to be sure your kids get enough of. Tired, cranky children can ruin a camping trip for the whole family.

Toddlers will be interested in animals, birds, leaves, flowers, rocks, stars, and other natural things. Try to share their interest. Maybe you'll both learn something.

Young children: The same kids who moan and groan about doing the chores at home can be efficient helpers at the campsite. Eager to please and capable of contributing to almost every campsite task—washing dishes, gathering wood, preparing meals, pitching the tent, and so on—small children can be very good campers.

They're getting to be good hikers, as well. With a miniature daypack and hiking boots, many a child will be proud to accompany you on the trails . . . for a short time, at least. Again, don't push them, but present them with tasks that will help them feel important and encourage them to continue. Show them the route on a map, and let them help identify landmarks and help navigate.

Safety is still an issue with small children, of course. Set campsite rules, and be sure to enforce them. Take precautions to prevent your child from getting lost if he or she wanders away.

Bring along plenty of games and toys, and don't forget a field guide or two as well to help them (and you) learn to identify flora and fauna indigenous to the area. Teach them bird calls. Help them learn about the natural world they're living in. Many kids this age look forward to an evening of storytelling and singing around the campfire before bed.

Solo flight, Buckskin Canyon, Utah.

Older kids and teenagers: Kids this age may feel that they've outgrown camping, or maybe they decide it just isn't cool. Able to help, they may be unwilling to pitch in. At this age, they may not be the good companions they used to be.

Parents who've been through this phase offer valuable counsel: Let the kids contribute to trip planning. If they help pick a place to go, they're more likely to enjoy themselves when they get there. If they plan the meal, they're more likely to cook it or clean up afterwards.

Allow plenty of time for older kids to go off on their own. Consider taking different dayhikes and meeting at the end of the day to compare notes before dinner. Don't leave your sense of humor at home.

One of the greatest pleasures of camping with older children is that you finally can leave the car behind again. Dust off your old backpack, rekindle your if-I-can't-carry-it-on-my-back-it's-not-coming spirit, and introduce your kids to the pure pleasures of the trail.

ON YOUR OWN

Every book on backpacking says not to hike alone, and every hiking club strictly advocates against the very notion of solo hiking. It's dangerous. What if you get hurt? What if you get lost?

True. Yet it's a fair bet that everyone who's ever written or spoken those words has then turned around and gone out hiking alone. Since we're not supposed to do it, we don't talk about it too much, but many people are willing to accept the risks inherent in solo hiking.

These people are usually contemplative individuals who want to hike for the solitude and quiet. They're not often the goal-oriented hikers, the ones who feel that they must hike faster and farther than anyone who has ever gone before them, or the ones for whom hitting the trails just means yelling and joking and drinking with their buddies in a rugged environment.

Solo hikers want to be able to stop when they want to stop and then go when they feel like it. They want to savor the sounds of nature unpolluted by the sounds of other hikers. They want to listen to the birds and the rustle of the leaves. They want to think, to reflect, not to make conversation.

Some hikers feel best sticking to dayhikes or overnights when they're going out on their own. Others will through-hike the Appalachian Trail with only the people they meet along the way for company.

To avoid trouble, they take certain simple precautions. The most important thing a solo hiker can do is leave a detailed note with a trustworthy person back home. The note should give as good an idea as possible about where you are going and when you expect to be back (allowing generously for delays). Include a list of what you're taking with you so that if you don't get home on schedule, the folks back home will be able to judge the degree of trouble you may be in.

If you're not familiar with the area, take some extra time to research its particular hazards—poisonous snakes, bears, and so on, so you'll know what you're getting into.

The other thing solo hikers take along with them in greater measure than do their more community-minded peers is a sense of caution. They check their gear extra-carefully before they leave. Many try to err on the side of caution, spending a lot more time looking for a safe way over that rushing brook or around that steep boulder than they would with a support system to fall back on. Rather than risk an accident, they might even turn back if a trail seems impassable. And they'd still savor the experience.

WOMEN ALONE

Did you read all the above thinking that we were talking about men, and men only? It's true—many people think that if it's foolhardy for a man to go out on his own, then it's downright dangerous for a woman to do it. So they assume no women do.

But able outdoorswomen, uncomfortable with being coddled, and as eager for solitude and challenges as any man, have proven over and over again that a woman's place is on the trail.

If they're nervous about who they meet along the way, they may make special efforts to walk aggressively, to refer to a male companion just around the bend if questioned, or simply avoid contact by staying off the trail when other people are around.

At day's end, they may make a point of seeking out a friendly group to camp near or they may turn their backs on other people entirely and look for a remote campsite off the beaten track and maintain their solitude.

Yes, there are cases of women hikers being assaulted. (There are also cases of men being assaulted.) But if a woman feels she can cope, there's nothing more than the risk of a little disapproval to stand in her way.

> WHEN SELECTING CLOTHING AND GEAR, BE AWARE THAT THERE'S A DIFFERENCE BE-TWEEN SMALL-SIZE MEN'S GEAR AND THAT WHICH IS SPECIFICALLY DESIGNED FOR A WOMAN'S BODY. THESE DAYS, CHOICES ABOUND, AND A WOMAN SHOULD NEVER HAVE TO SETTLE FOR A PACK WHOSE FRAME DIGS INTO HER HIPS OR A JACKET THAT'S TIGHT ACROSS THE CHEST AND LONG IN THE ARMS.

A hike of her own.

© Bob Winsett/Tom Stack & Associates

WITH MORE AND MORE WOMEN ENJOYING THE OUTDOORS, A PUBLICATION HAS BEEN STARTED UP JUST FOR THEM. CONTACT *OUTDOOR WOMAN*, P.O. BOX 834, NYACK, NY 10960.

Leaving the world behind.

WOMEN TOGETHER

Most women who go backpacking generally do so with other people, especially if it's going to be an overnighter.

But many women never even go at all not realizing what a fulfilling, exciting time they could have. Their husbands and boyfriends invite them along, and they say, "Not me—I had enough of that in the Girl Scouts."

Fair enough. But a closed mind is a dangerous thing. Many a woman with that attitude has been pleasantly surprised in the outdoors once she's analyzed and learned to cope with her fears.

Many women fear that they won't be able to carry a backpack. They have weak shoulders, they complain. True. Women's upper body muscles are weaker than men's. But since a well-fitting pack with a hipbelt will put the bulk of the pack's weight over the woman's hips and legs—where they are strong— that argument doesn't really hold water. But there are two caveats—the pack must be well-fitting. It cannot just be any old pack at all; it must be tailored for a woman's smaller torso and frame. And women, as much as men, have to keep their expectations reasonable. They must be in good physical condition before setting off with a pack on their backs, or they'll soon be back home vowing, "Never again."

Women should be aware, however, that no matter how strong and capable they may be, men may prove to be faster walkers. You don't have to compete with them. Remember, not only are most men's legs longer, but they've got a substantially higher percentage of muscle in their bodies (40 percent) than women do (23 percent). Women often decide to walk by themselves at their own pace, meeting the men in the group at some predetermined spot. This way, everyone is happier.

Some women are unwilling to put up with a certain amount of discomfort. Well, if comfort is what you're looking for, backpacking isn't your sport. But do consider that a warm sleeping bag on top of a soft pad inside of a cozy tent isn't all that bad. Particularly after a long day of exercise and fresh air and beautiful scenery.

What about bugs? Insect repellent works as well on the trail as it does on the veranda. Also, if you're particularly sensitive to insect bites, even allergic, make sure you dress appropriately—long sleeves, long pants, socks, all liberally doused with bug juice if necessary—and consider even acquiring a head net if you think it'll help.

Snakes? The thing about snakes is that they're a lot less interested in seeing you than you should be in seeing them. They'll always try to avoid contact with a human being, and will only attack if they feel cornered. So don't corner them. Find out about what kinds of snakes (especially poisonous ones) exist in your area. Learn to recognize their preferred habitat—in dense underbrush, amid big rocks and fallen trees. Look where you're going, and don't put your hand or foot into a crevice that could be a snake's hideaway. If you see one, back off, and let it get away in peace. Also, never travel deep into snake country without a snakebite kit.

Some women have an aversion to dirt. There's no denying it—you get dirty on the trail. Try an overnight first to see how it feels to wash your face in water from a stream and pull your hair back to keep it out of your way. You might find it liberating. Many women do.

Many women find other things liberating about backpacking. They find, for example, that some traditional sex roles are erased once the dinner has to be cooked outside. Women aren't automatically expected to do all of the cooking and washing—in fact, many times they have to fight to be permitted to be an equal participant in the chores. For some reason, men who've never learned how to turn on the stove at home are self-professed experts at camp cooking. So, by all means, don't try to stop them.

WOMEN WITHOUT A BATHROOM

We've said elsewhere that you shouldn't use toilet paper in the woods. You probably read that thinking, "That's easy for a man to say." But the fact is, one of us is a woman, neither of us likes that rule, but both of us accept it. Haven't you ever noticed wads and streamers of toilet paper decorating previous camp latrines? What a terrible way to leave your mark on the wilderness. So when we use toilet paper, we use it sparingly and stash it in plastic bags to be packed out or burned.

The other thing for women to be prepared for is menstruation. If you're at all likely to get your period during the time you'll be out in the woods, you probably will. Bring tampons or pads—whatever you use—but bring plenty of plastic bags and a small metal box to store the used ones in. You really can't toss these things in a campfire—they don't burn very well—and you can't bury them either, leaving them there until animals, attracted by the smell of blood, dig them up. Pack it out.

> MANY WOMEN FIND THAT THEIR SKILLS IMPROVE AND THEIR CONFIDENCE AND ENJOYMENT OF THE OUTDOORS ARE ENHANCED WHEN THEY GO BACKPACKING WITHOUT MEN. RECOGNIZING THIS, MANY HIKING CLUBS OFFER OUTINGS FOR WOMEN ONLY, AND GROUPS LIKE OUTWARD BOUND PROVIDE THEM WITH MORE ADVENTUROUS SINGLE-SEX CHALLENGES AS WELL.

This backpacker has chosen to go it alone, finding solitude as challenging as it is liberating and enlightening.

If you do get your period on the trail, by the way, try not to schedule particularly arduous hikes during this time. You may feel sluggish and tired. Don't feel like you have to make yourself hit the trail, or it simply won't be as enjoyable. It's easier—and smarter—just to accept it and take it easy for a few days than to fight Mother Nature.

There's been a lot of talk about the safety of a menstruating woman in grizzly bear country. Some people think that the grizzlies, attracted by the smell of blood, pose such a danger that women should simply avoid the backcountry during their periods. There are no hard and fast rules about this—as with most things concerning grizzly behavior—but it is something to think about.

WITH A DOG

We were alone on a trail in New York State on a beautiful clear fall day. It had been hours since we'd seen another soul, and we were walking quietly, looking at birds, catching the occasional glimpse of a deer, and admiring the foliage.

Then, suddenly, there was the sound of a galloping herd approaching, getting louder and louder, and coming right at us through the underbrush. Before we had time to get out of the way, two huge German shepherds came tumbling out of the woods at our feet, chasing each other, and having a fine old time.

Now, we like dogs as much as the next person, but at that moment those two dogs—and their owner—were not tops on our hit parade. They'd startled us badly and destroyed our placid mood, not to mention scaring off all the wildlife in the vicinity. At that moment, we would have gladly supported a permanent ban on all dogs on all trails in all places on the planet. And the ban would have been ratified by the countless canine-less campers who've been kept awake by others' barking dogs or bothered by the sound of their owners calling them.

But still there are dogs (and owners) who are pleasures to meet on the trail. They're the ones who are considerate enough to abide by the rules. (Rules? Rules. There actually are rules, you know. In some places, such as national parks, it's illegal to hike with a dog, and in those places where it is permitted, you've usually got to keep the dog on a leash.) If all dog owners were responsible and thoughtful and showed some sensitivity to the rights of other hikers, there probably wouldn't be any controversy at all.

© John Flannery/Visuals Unlimited

There are packs designed especially for dogs that enable them to carry their own food and water on the trail.

C H A P T E R N I N E

Mowich Lake, Mt. Rainier National Park: the perfect picture of tranquillity.

U.S. AND CANADA

THE BIG THREE

While most hikers choose to (or have to) settle for dayhikes, overnights, or—at most—a week's backpack here or there, the lucky few are more ambitious. They can take some time after graduation, between jobs, or just whenever the urge arises, and devote a few months to a special goal: hiking the length of one of North America's Big Three—the Appalachian, Pacific Crest, and Continental Divide trails.

The following should provide all essential information for those hikers who hope to hike an entire trail (or more!), those for whom a short section is enough, and those who simply want to dream.

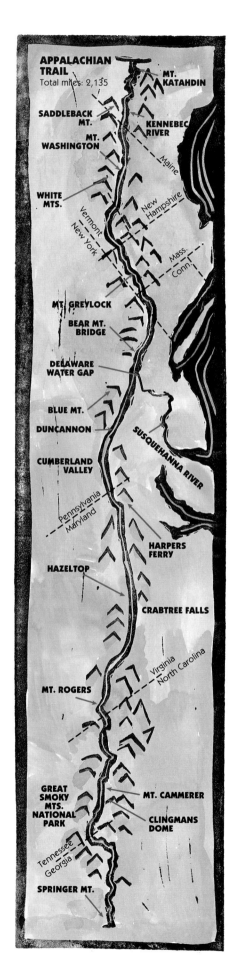

APPALACHIAN TRAIL
Total miles: 2,135

MT. KATAHDIN
SADDLEBACK MT.
KENNEBEC RIVER
MT. WASHINGTON
Maine
WHITE MTS.
New Hampshire
Vermont
New York
Mass.
Conn.
MT. GREYLOCK
BEAR MT. BRIDGE
DELAWARE WATER GAP
BLUE MT.
DUNCANNON
SUSQUEHANNA RIVER
CUMBERLAND VALLEY
Pennsylvania
Maryland
HARPERS FERRY
HAZELTOP
CRABTREE FALLS
Virginia
North Carolina
MT. ROGERS
GREAT SMOKY MTS. NATIONAL PARK
MT. CAMMERER
CLINGMANS DOME
Tennessee
Georgia
SPRINGER MT.

APPALACHIAN TRAIL: THE WORLD'S MOST FAMOUS BACKPACK

Stretching 2,135 miles from Springer Mountain, Georgia, to the top of Mount Katahdin in Maine, the venerable Appalachian Trail must be the most traveled long trail on earth. Every year, nearly a thousand people attempt to hike the entire length of the AT (although only a fraction make it all the way), while thousands more undertake shorter treks ranging in length from daytrips to weeks-long excursions.

Don't hike large sections of the AT if you're expecting endless mountainous challenges. (The Pacific Crest and Continental Divide Trails await.) Much of the AT's route, particularly those portions in the mid-Atlantic states, passes through gentle, rolling countryside.

At either end of the trail, however, more spectacular scenery (and a greater roadblock to a through-hike) exists. The trek through the Great Smoky Mountains in Tennessee can produce severe weather, slippery slopes, one tiring uphill and downhill scramble after another—and rewards like the spectacular view of Mount Kammerer, one of the East Coast's least-known scenic glories. Similarly, the White Mountains in New Hampshire, the "100-Mile Wilderness" in Maine (as untouched as any countryside in the Northeast), and the final climb up Mount Katahdin provide glorious challenges.

For more information on the Appalachian Trail, contact the Appalachian Trail Conference, P.O. Box 807, Harpers Ferry, West Virginia 25425.

CONTINENTAL DIVIDE TRAIL: SPLITTING THE COUNTRY

While every casual backpacker at least knows about the Appalachian Trail, remarkably few have even the slightest inkling about the 2,650-mile Continental Divide Trail. This magnificent trail begins in the deserts of New Mexico, wends its way through some of the most spectacular mountain country in North America, and lets out at the Montana–Canada border in Glacier–Waterton Lakes National Parks.

Fewer than 10 people a year through-hike the entire CDT, for a very good reason: Like the other two long trails, the entire route takes a good six months to hike, which means that you're guaranteed to run into severe winter weather at one end of the trail or the other. (And there are no shelters, a shock to those expecting the creature comforts of the AT.)

Whether you're through-hiking or not, the CDT will take you through some of the most pristine wilderness in all of North America. Backpacking through the San Juan Mountains in southern Colorado (average elevation: 11,500 feet); past the glimmering alpine lakes of Wyoming's magnificent Wind River Mountains; and across the 100-plus roadless miles of Bob Marshall Wilderness in Montana (home to elk, bobcat, and grizzly bear), you'll have a chance to get an incomparable close-up view of the magnificent scenery of the mountain states.

For more information, contact the Continental Divide Trail Coordinator, Forest Service, P.O. Box 25127, Lakewood, Colorado 80225, or the Continental Divide Trail Society, P.O. Box 30002, Bethesda, Maryland 20814.

CONTINENTAL DIVIDE TRAIL
Total Miles: 2,650

© Sharon Gerig/Tom Stack & Associates

Previous page: Backpackers on the spectacular Paintbrush Canyon Trail in Grand Teton National Park, Wyoming. Below, top: Black bear cub. Below, bottom: Mt. Shuksan, North Cascades National Park, Washington, the end of the trail. Opposite page: Anza-Borrego Desert State Park, the trailhead of the Pacific Crest Trail.

THE PACIFIC CREST TRAIL: FROM DESERT TO MOUNTAINTOP

Stick to the AT if you need to cross as many states as possible on your through-hike. But if you want an unmatched view of California's natural glories, as well as some of Oregon and Washington's finest mountain scenery, backpack almost any portion of the 2,627-mile PCT.

Like the CDT, this spectacular trail begins in the hot deserts of the southwest—in this case, California's Anza-Borrego Desert State Park, hard by the Mexican border.

Much of the rest of the PCT takes you along, beside, and over the crest's endless mountain ranges. You'll cross the San Andreas Fault, skirt the blistering Mojave Desert, and cross Forester Pass (elevation: 13,180 feet) in southern California; likely encounter inquisitive black bears in Kings Canyon and Sequoia National Parks; keep an eye peeled for snowstorms any month of the year in the Sierra Nevada Mountains; glimpse the wonders of Yosemite National Park (and perhaps stay awhile); and join the Cascade Range in northern California.

The volcanic origin of the Cascades is immediately apparent as you make your way through Oregon and Washington. In Oregon are the tourist-trap Crater Lake National Park, evidence of a vast ancient eruption; the little-known

PACIFIC CREST TRAIL
Total miles: 2,627

MANNING PROVINCIAL PARK

NORTH CASCADES NATIONAL PARK

LAKE CHELAN

GLACIER PEAK

MT. RAINIER NATIONAL PARK

Washington

MT. ADAMS

COLUMBIA RIVER

MT. HOOD

CASCADE RANGE

JEFFERSON PARK

MT. JEFFERSON

THREE SISTERS VOLCANOS

CRATER LAKE NATIONAL PARK

SKY LAKES

Oregon
California

MT. SHASTA

LASSEN PARK

MARBLE MT.   TRINITY ALPS

LAKE TAHOE

DESOLATION WILDERNESS

TUOLUMNE MEADOWS

YOSEMITE NATIONAL PARK

SIERRA NEVADA

KINGS CANYON and SEQUOIA NATIONAL PARK

FORESTER PASS

MT. WHITNEY

MOJAVE DESERT

MT. BADEN POWELL

SAN ANDREAS FAULT

SAN JACINTO PEAK

ANZA-BORREGO DESERT STATE PARK

CAMPO

Three Sisters Volcanoes; and the spectacular Jefferson Park. The Washington section boasts such famous volcanoes as Mount Adams and unparalleled glimpses of Mount Rainier. For a view of northwest scenery at its apex, spend some extra time in North Cascades National Park, just south of the Canadian border and the end of the trail.

For more information, contact the Pacific Crest Trail Coordinator, Pacific Northwest Regional Office, Forest Service, 319 S.W. Pine Street, Portland, Oregon 97208, or the Pacific Crest Trail Conference, 365 W. 29th Ave, Eugene, Oregon 97405.

SMALLER GLORIES

Even the world's most dedicated hiker could not navigate every mile of trail laid out in the United States and Canada—a fact that is frustrating to the compulsive completist, but a source of joy and wonder to the rest of us. Despite a growing population, rampant logging, and explosive development in many areas, North America remains a blessedly empty continent—particularly if you avoid the most heavily visited parks and head for less-traveled wilderness areas. You might be surprised by how satisfied you will be with a less-than-famous trail.

Whether you're searching for starry desert nights, mountain treks, walks through misty forests, or strolls down empty beaches, it's still possible to spend days hiking with only yourself, the local flora and fauna, and the scenery for company.

The following list (which concentrates on less familiar destinations) should give a hint of the glories still to be hiked close to home.

Hint, by the way, is the operative word here. There's nowhere near enough room to go into further detail and still be relatively comprehensive. For more information, contact the National Forest Service or the parks department of the appropriate states.

If you're interested in learning about the hiking and camping possibilities in the national parks, contact the National Park Service (or, of course, the parks themselves). For a head start, turn to page 170 for a list of many organizations in the United States and Canada to call or write for further information. We chose not to discuss the national parks here; they've been well covered in many other books.

MOUNTAINS AND CANYONS

ARIZONA: CHIRICAHUA MOUNTAINS

Little visited, filled with extraordinary scenery and even more spectacular contrasts, southeastern Arizona is a treat for the knowledgeable hiker. The jagged Chiricahuas, set in the Coronado National Forest, rise from the endless mesquite deserts like ancient monuments; enter them, and you'll come upon a shockingly cool new world, framed by red-rock canyons and capped with dense pine forests, that contains fascinating birds and animals found only here and in Mexico.

Balancing rock, Chiricahua National Monument.

The bald eagle soars high over many North American national parks.

© Thomas Kitchin/Tom Stack & Associates

A lone bighorn sheep, looking almost frozen, on a snowy mountainside.

© Thomas Kitchen/Tom Stack & Associates

ARKANSAS: OZARK NATIONAL FOREST

Drive northwest from Little Rock for about an hour and a half, and you'll find yourself in a vast, misty forest, set amid odd, crumbling limestone and sandstone rock formations. This is the one-million-acre Ozark National Forest, a unique forest that has grown atop an ancient seabed. The many trails here provide access to some of the least explored wilderness in the entire region. Watch for bears, birds, and even the occasional fossil!

BRITISH COLUMBIA: THE STRATHCONA HIGH RIDGES

You don't usually think of islands as being good places for mountain hikes, but enormous Vancouver is an island with a difference. Lush and mountainous, largely unsettled and undisturbed, Vancouver provides some of the best upland hiking in Canada. The Strathcona High Ridges (which reach five thousand feet in elevation) are a continuing pleasure: Treeless snowfields, meadows alight with alpine wildflowers, views of nearby mountains, and abundant birdlife are all here.

CALIFORNIA: JOHN MUIR WILDERNESS

Courtright Reservoir, east of Fresno, provides the gateway to some of the High Sierra's most stunning scenery. Glorious mountain passes, glistening peaks, sparkling cascades, days spent above ten thousand feet—all are available in this superb wilderness, a dream for any mountain hiker. And when you're done here, try one of thousands of other trails that dot the magnificent Sierras.

CALIFORNIA: SANTA LUCIA MOUNTAINS

California boasts many mountain ranges, but the coastal ranges (which include the Santa Lucias) are certainly among the most beautiful. The almost endless hiking alternatives here will bring you past redwood forests, through rugged canyons, and to the tops of jagged ridges where, suddenly, you'll come upon spectacular views of the great Pacific.

COLORADO: COLLEGIATE PEAKS

For a view of an Ivy League you've probably never heard of before, take a trip to Colorado's Sawatch Mountains, home to fifteen peaks higher than fourteen thousand feet. Here you'll find a trio of mountains named after early explorers and surveyors: Yale, Harvard, and Columbia, three of the great fifteen. All are terrific challenges, but none require mountaineering expertise to ascend.

Below Mt. Yale, Collegiate Peaks.

© Stuart M. Green/Tom Stack & Associates

Opposite page: Maroon Bells, Colorado.

COLORADO: MAROON BELLS

You could spend a lifetime hiking Colorado's mountains, but you'd have a hard time finding a lovelier route than the Maroon-Snowmass Trail, surprisingly near the bright lights of Aspen. If you need something to do in between skiing seasons, the trail's views of the picture-perfect, snowcapped Maroon Bells should provide a perfect alternative.

HAWAII: HALEAKALA VOLCANO

Imagine spending days backpacking through the barren, steamy interior of a dormant volcano, then hiking downslope through jungles filled with colorful birds, and ending up on an exquisite beach that's perfect for swimming and snorkeling. If this sounds good, start making arrangements to visit Maui's Haleakala Volcano, one of the finest wilderness trips on the Hawaiian Islands.

North rim, Haleakala.

© Jack D. Swenson/Tom Stack & Associates

IDAHO AND OREGON: HELL'S CANYON NATIONAL RECREATION AREA

More than five hundred thousand acres of high mountain passes, rocky canyons, and the Snake River, Hell's Canyon remains a neglected destination by many hikers (though not by river rafters). If you want to join the chosen few, consider walking the thirty-one-mile Snake River national recreation trail—particularly beautiful during the wildflower show in spring.

© John D. Cunningham/Visuals Unlimited

MICHIGAN: THE PORCUPINES

Mountains in Michigan? Well, Summit Peak, the highest in the Porcupine Range, doesn't quite reach two thousand feet—and it's the highest point in the whole region. But if you're willing to skip snow-capped peaks, then the virgin hemlock forests, clear ponds, and icy streams of this undisturbed wilderness (nestled next to Lake Superior) are reward enough.

NEW HAMPSHIRE: THE WHITE MOUNTAINS

The great Whites are without a doubt the most dramatic and challenging mountains in the northeast—and the Presidential Range is the peak of the Whites. Home to hidden lakes and streams, spectacular views, and an extensive trail system, Mounts Washington, Eisenhower, and Adams are an exciting destination for the serious backpacker.

Opposite page: Franconia Ridge, White Mountains, New Hampshire. Above: Another way to see Mt. Washington.

© Jack D. Swenson/Tom Stack & Associates

Fall colors, Adirondacks.

A world of choices: the High Peaks.

NEW YORK: THE HIGH PEAKS

New York's Adirondack Mountains may be gentler and lower than many others, but they can also boast some of the most pristine, verdant scenery on earth. The High Peaks region comprises forty-six peaks above four thousand feet, with Mt. Marcy the highest at 5,344 feet. Hike up this mountain or another of the High Peaks during the fall, and you'll be treated to a foliage show so spectacular that it may leave you breathless.

Below: Young black-tailed deer.

ONTARIO: KILLARNEY PROVINCIAL PARK

Some of the best hiking—and most precious solitude—in Canada can be found in the provincial parks. The 120,000-acre Killarney is a perfect example, a gorgeous landscape of lakes, forests, and the white quartzite La Cloche Mountains, hidden in southeastern Ontario. Try the sixty-two-mile La Cloche Silhouette Trail, which ascends to Silver Peak, the park's highest point.

PENNSYLVANIA: TIOGA STATE FOREST

Hidden in the north-central part of the state, less than three hundred miles from Philadelphia, Cleveland, and Washington D.C., the 160,000-acre Tioga contains some of the most surprising and exciting geography in eastern North America. Here lies the Pennsylvania Grand Canyon, a five-hundred-foot-deep gorge carved over millennia by Pine Creek. Come here for spectacular views, the thickest forest in the entire mid-Atlantic, abundant wildlife, and few people—a treasure in the heavily populated northeast.

QUEBEC: LAURENTIDES PARK

One of Quebec's largest parks, Laurentides also contains some of the most rugged, remote, and unexplored terrain on the continent. The hiker here will find endless boreal forests—and the moose, bear, otters, and other animals that make these forests their home—but, even more importantly, will catch a glimpse of the marvelous wildness that still possesses so much of Canada's open spaces.

© Thomas Kitchin/Tom Stack & Associates

Black bear do their fishing in Laurentides Park, Quebec.

© Dick Poe/Visuals Unlimited

The misty Green Mountains, Vermont.

VERMONT: THE GREENS

For all its booming ski resorts, much of Vermont remains a hilly, forested wilderness. Among the most pristine areas left is the fifteen-thousand-acre Lye Brook Wilderness in the south-central Green Mountains. Watch for warblers and other nesting birds in summer, porcupines and other mammals (including a moose, if you're lucky) at any time of the year, and a sense of peace and tranquility that even Thoreau would have approved of.

WASHINGTON: THE NORTH CASCADES

Yes, the North Cascades is a national park, and shouldn't be on this list. But the Stehekin Valley is accessible only by a three-hour ferry across frigid Lake Chelan, and thus is remote and little-visited enough to qualify. It's also worth the trip. The towering, jagged North Cascades are among the most beautiful mountains on the continent, and the snowy mountain passes, glacial lakes, evergreen forests, waterfalls, and wildflowers make for a premiere hiking treat.

DESERT JAUNTS

ARIZONA:
ORGAN PIPE CACTUS NATIONAL MONUMENT

Nestled on the Arizona-Mexico border, at the juncture of three different deserts, lies one of the country's most fascinating preserves. Within its spacious boundaries lies the remote, unspoiled Organ Pipe Wilderness, more than 300,000 acres of remarkably verdant desert landscape.

The show is at its peak in February, when Organ Pipe's golden poppies, lupines, lilies, and other flowers burst into a sustained wildflower show— stunning to anyone with a preconceived notion of what a desert should look like—that lasts well into March.

The namesake of Organ Pipe Cactus National Monument.

Opposite page: The blooming desert of Joshua Tree National Monument. Left: Anza-Borrego State Park.

CALIFORNIA: ANZA-BORREGO STATE PARK

Forty miles from San Diego, just southwest of the barren Salton Sea, this little-known park protects a thousand-square-mile section of upland (and therefore comparatively cool) desert. It's a wonderful place to stumble upon Indian pictographs; wake on a crisp morning to the dawn chorus of quail, doves, and wrens; and capture (either on film or in your mind's eye) views of the Vallecito, Fish Creek, and Santa Rosa Mountains.

CALIFORNIA:
JOSHUA TREE NATIONAL MONUMENT

A more typical desert environment, this southern California preserve receives less than five inches of rain a year. This is the arid home of cholla and prickly pear, lizards darting under every rock, rattlesnakes (if you look for them), jackrabbits turning their satellite-dish ears in your direction, coyotes ambling away, and eagles soaring on thermals far overhead.

Joshua Tree.

© David Matherly/Visuals Unlimited

NEVADA: RUBY MOUNTAINS

The desert mountains remain among the most inaccessible in North America; far too often one can only gaze at them yearningly from the arid lowlands, wishing for an extra month's hiking time. On the other hand, those that are easier to explore tend to draw crowds of hikers who can't get enough of the desert. The Ruby Mountains, whose northern edge nearly touches I-80, provide an unspoiled alternative. Consider taking the forty-three-mile Ruby Crest Trail; the opening ten miles draw crowds, but after that it should be just you and the pristine Nevada landscape.

WYOMING: THE WIND RIVER MOUNTAINS

Can any range have a more evocative, haunting name than the Wind River Mountains in western Wyoming? Luckily, this beautiful wilderness area lives up to its name, boasting trout-filled lakes, canyons bordered by alpine meadows alive with flowers, and abundant wildlife. Try the Down's Lake and Ross Lake Trails—or blaze your own trails in the challenging Down's Fork area.

THE GREAT DUNES

MICHIGAN:
SLEEPING BEAR DUNES NATIONAL LAKESHORE

Imagine Lake Michigan, and you may find yourself thinking of cities, factories, Detroit—anything but a marvelously beautiful wilderness featuring some of the highest sand dunes on earth.

Welcome to Sleeping Bear, a 71,000-acre preserve that protects twenty of the last unspoiled miles of lakeshore. Here are dunes that sprout almost from the lake itself and stand as high as 460 feet. Tear yourself away from these spectacular monuments, and you'll find that the preserve also boasts unpolluted lakes, free-flowing streams, and forests that host more than two hundred species of nesting and migrating birds.

OREGON:
OREGON DUNES NATIONAL RECREATION AREA

Just an hour's drive from Eugene lies this 32,000-acre reserve, which protects forty miles of prime coastline and the West Coast's most extensive system of dunes. For the best backpacking, head for the Tahkenitch Trail or the Umpqua Dunes Scenic Area—but anywhere in the area will give you a sense of the endless appeal of the Pacific coast.

Sunrise at Baker Beach Dunes.

A rocky river in Vancouver Island, British Columbia.

HITTING THE BEACHES

BRITISH COLUMBIA: VANCOUVER ISLAND

Though the West Coast Trail is part of the popular Pacific Rim National Park, this forty-five-mile stretch of wilderness coastline remains almost unvisited. The trail itself (which lies just outside the park) was first designed as a "life-saving trail," cut through the dense coastal forest to provide rescue routes for the countless people whose ships sank on the treacherous rocks offshore. Today, only totally self-sufficient backpackers, fully provisioned and willing to be stranded by rough weather for days at a time, brave the harsh—but extraordinarily beautiful—forests and beaches of this section of the park.

© Robert Lankinen/The Wildlife Collection

CALIFORNIA: THE LOST COAST

North of San Francisco lies one of the most beautiful and unspoiled stretches of beach in the world—and almost no one knows about it. Backed by the stormy, four thousand-foot King Mountains, untrammeled by roads, the black-sand beaches of the Lost Coast provide a challenging twenty-five-mile hike that can take two days or as long as you want.

Watch for sea lions cavorting on offshore rocks; freshwater streams emptying into the placid ocean; the occasional timber from a long-sunk ship; and ancient Indian middens left by the tribes that once harvested the waters off of this glorious coast.

HAWAII: BIG ISLAND

Not every Hawaiian beach is lined with hotels and condos, with perfectly tanned bodies, redolent of suntan lotion, packed flank-to-flank. Backpackers have a better option: the windward side of the Big Island, home to rugged hills, dense forests that hide sparkling waterfalls, and black-sand beaches accessible only by foot.

Silver sword in bloom, Hawaii.

MAINE: ISLE AU HAUT

Almost everyone visits Acadia National Park, and no wonder—its headlands, forests, and rocky beaches are stunningly beautiful. They're also way overcrowded every summer, unless you forget the busiest areas and ride the mail boat to Isle Au Haut.

Don't go expecting vast wilderness; there are under twenty miles of trails on the island. What you will find is easy access to the Maine coast (so often inaccessible, in private hands), as well as the peaceful fir and spruce woodlands that border the rocky beaches.

NEW BRUNSWICK: MISCOU AND LAMEQUE ISLANDS

These two little-known islands form Land's End of New Brunswick, and they retain all the charm of unspoiled harbors, marshes, and beaches. The bird-watching here is nothing short of spectacular, the beaches rocky and wind-swept (make a special point of visiting Plage de l'Ouest on Miscou), and the sense of peace—of being almost off the edge of the modern world—is incomparable.

TEXAS: SOUTH PADRE ISLAND

Opposite page: Padre Island National Seashore.

South Padre Island is, in reality, little more than a ridge of dunes bordered by beaches. Just thirty-four miles in length, it has been left blessedly free of condos, hotel resorts, and endless shingled houses. Instead, much of the island remains a wild, roadless paradise, scoured by wind and pounded by constant surf.

Backpack here and you'll find roseate spoonbills, black skimmers, and other fascinating birds; countless shells; floats from Japanese fishing boats; and perhaps even a gold coin from one of the treasures of gold bullion lost in shipwrecks offshore.

Live oaks thrive on South Padre Island.

VIRGINIA, NORTH AND SOUTH CAROLINA: THE OUTER BANKS

Most famous as the home of the Wright Brothers, the Outer Banks actually have a far more colorful and detailed maritime history. Hundreds of miles of islands built of shifting sand, the Outer Banks incorporate several National Seashores and Wildlife Refuges containing miles of trails. But these wonderful beaches also provide a haunting sense of the impermanence of time; everywhere are vestiges of drowned houses, sunken ships, and even a crumbling highway, all of which have succumbed to the relentless Atlantic.

WASHINGTON: NORTH WILDERNESS COAST

The wildest section of Olympic National Park's Pacific Coast section, this hike—which leads north from Rialto Beach, near the town of La Push—provides a bouquet of everything that makes the northern Pacific coast so stunning. The surf crashes against the coarse black-sand beach; pine-topped sea stacks loom offshore; cormorants and shearwaters wheel above the horizon; and driftwood logs one hundred feet long or longer lie scattered along the beach like a giant's toothpicks.

This is a wilderness hike to make you forget about civilization. But don't forget your tide table—high tide renders many headlands impassable, and foolish hikers have been trapped or killed.

Shi-shi Beach, Olympic National Park.

FLATLANDS: MARSHES AND PLAINS

Sea stacks, Olympic National Park.

CALIFORNIA: THE CARRIZO PLAIN

Set in the state's fertile, heavily framed Central Valley, the recently established 180,000-acre Carrizo Plain preserves some of the last vestiges of prairie that once covered the entire valley. A refuge for rare flora and fauna (including the kit fox and sandhill crane), the plain was protected through a unique cooperative effort between oil companies, local ranchers, government agencies, and, of course, conservation organizations. Visit it for its beauty, its abundant wildlife—and also for an encouraging glimpse of a possible way to protect other fragile areas in the future.

Pawnee National Grassland.

© Berry Conway/Tom Stack & Associates

COLORADO: PAWNEE NATIONAL GRASSLAND

Head east from the Rockies and you'll soon enter a part of Colorado few outsiders even know exists: vast high plains dotted with monumental buttes that cover 34,000 square miles of this otherwise mountainous state. As has been the fate of so much North American prairieland, much of Colorado's other shortgrass has been converted to farms and rangeland.

Dominated by East and West Pawnee Buttes (the latter is more than five hundred feet tall), these dry grasslands give visitors a chance to view the daunting horizons, enormous sky, and endless flatlands that greeted the first pioneers little more than a century ago.

FLORIDA: BIG CYPRESS NATIONAL PRESERVE

Just forty-five miles west of Miami lies this seven-hundred-thousand-acre preserve, which contains abundant wetlands, slash pine groves, fields of sawgrass, and—of course—ancient, massive cypresses. Come here to escape the bustle of the big city and the plastic of the strip malls and instead spot birds, snakes, and other Florida wildlife specialties, or hike part of the new Florida Scenic Trail (see page 127), which crosses the preserve for thirty-eight of its thirteen hundred miles.

THE FAR NORTH

ALASKA:
THE ARCTIC NATIONAL WILDLIFE REFUGE

Frequently called "North America's Serengeti," the ANWR (still threatened by oil exploitation) boasts some of the most spectacular tundra and mountain scenery on the continent. Here are opportunities to follow the great caribou herds as they make their age-old migration in search of food. Without a doubt, it's one of the world's great wildlife spectacles.

Go in June, and you'll avoid (most) biting insects and be able to take advantage of the brief but vivid tundra wildflower show, the abundance of nesting birds, and the sight of musk-oxen, grizzlies, and perhaps even a pack of tundra wolves.

ALASKA: CHILKOOT TRAIL

In 1896, miners found gold near Dawson City in the Yukon, sparking one of the last great gold rushes. Thousands of fortune-hunters gathered in the Alaskan coastal city of Skagway, then fought their way over a rough mountain trail to the goldfields. Today, backpackers can trace the steps of last century's stampeders on a week-long backpack along the Chilkoot Trail, past abandoned shacks, camps, and caches untouched since the rush. Don't expect to find much gold, though—it's long gone.

© Larry Lipsky/Tom Stack & Associates

Black-necked stilt, Big Cypress Swamp.

YUKON: BAFFIN ISLAND

The scenic and wildlife opportunities are almost endless on this huge island, which sprawls across the Arctic Circle 1,500 miles north of Montreal. Backpackers trek beneath granite walls that tower more than a mile above them; hike past frigid, gleaming glacial lakes; and explore the great expanses of Penny Glacier, a true polar icecap.

Tundra, Baffin Island.

© Pat Armstrong/Visuals Unlimited

YUKON: ELLESMERE ISLAND

Due north of Baffin Island, hard by the western coast of Greenland, this virtually unexplored island is one of the most northerly landmasses on earth. The lucky visitor here will find surprisingly lush valleys (home to nesting birds and ponderous musk-oxen, as well as the more expected (and breathtakingly spectacular) glaciers, fjords, icecaps, and tundra.

NEW LONG TRAILS: COMING SOON TO A WILDERNESS NEAR YOU

If the past decade's hiking boom has had a single valuable effect, it's been to mobilize local and national hiking groups, environmental organizations, and even the federal government to create a handful of new long trails to accompany the Big Three. Some are still in the dreaming stage, while others are nearly complete—but all will provide unparalleled access to the mountains, waterways, and forests that remain wild and unspoiled in North America.

Our prescription for itchy feet: Read the following, lace up your hiking boots, and hit the trail.

AMERICAN DISCOVERY TRAIL

Route: Trailhead: Point Reyes National Seashore near San Francisco.

Terminus: Prime Hook National Wildlife Refuge, on the Delaware coast.

Distance: 5,500 miles.

First envisioned by the American Hiking Society, and currently also supported by *Backpacker* magazine, the American Discovery Trail has been designed to link the Appalachian Trail, the Continental Divide, and the Pacific Crest Trail—and also connect thirty thousand miles of previously existing trails across the continent. When complete, the route will pass through California sagebrush, Nevada desert, Utah salt flats, the Rockies in Colorado, the plains of Nebraska, Illinois, and Iowa, and on into the gentler terrain of the eastern seaboard.

In 1992, Rodale Press (publisher of *Backpacker*) will release a trail map and guidebook to the American Discovery Trail.

FLORIDA SCENIC TRAIL

Route: Trailhead: the Everglades.

Terminus: the western Panhandle.

Distance: 1,300 miles.

Most long trails—both established and proposed—seem almost to be in competition for most ambitious route. ("How many states does *your* trail cover? Fifteen? Well, *mine* includes deserts, mountains, virgin forests, and the ocean. Match that!")

The nearly complete Florida Scenic Trail is different than most long trails. It aims only to show hikers a Florida far from the beach resorts, the endless baking highways, the Spring Break crowds. Follow this trail, and you'll watch herons, egrets, and other birds stalk marshy shallows; walk through sawgrass meadows; play hide-and-seek with ten-foot alligators; relax in shady oak hammocks; and return with an indelible impression of how beautiful and mysterious Florida used to be.

Following pages: Grand Canyon.

A glorious sunset adorns this pine tree in the Everglades National Park, Florida.

© Doug Sokell/Visuals Unlimited

The spectacular rock formations on Bryce Canyon National Park in Utah leave most backpackers speechless.

GREAT WESTERN TRAIL

Route: Trailhead: the Idaho-British Columbia border.

Terminus: the Mexican border of Arizona.

Distance: 2,400 miles.

Passing through twenty national forests, sneaking along the border of six national parks and twelve national monuments, and hooking up with such historic trails as the one used by Lewis and Clark, the Great Western Trail (due to be completed in 1995, but mostly usable now) takes hikers through some of the most spectacular scenery in all of North America.

Among the extraordinarily varied highlights of this rugged trail are the remote forests of Idaho's River of No Return Wilderness Area; the Wasatch Mountains of Utah (where the trail makes its way up and finally reaches more than eleven thousand feet in elevation); the otherworldly rock formations of Bryce Canyon; the spectacular north rim of the Grand Canyon, which seems to look different at every moment; and the Catalina Mountains of southern Arizona. Every mile reveals another remarkable vista.

NORTH COUNTRY TRAIL

Route: Trailhead: near Lake Champlain, New York.

Terminus: Lake Sakakawea, North Dakota.

Distance: 3,200 miles.

You might think it difficult to create a scenic trail through such heavily populated states as New York, Ohio, Michigan, and Minnesota, but the designers and funders of the North Country Trail (including the National Forest Service and several local volunteer organizations) rose to the challenge. The result is a trail that reveals a slew of little-known glories of the North American landscape.

The trail begins in the lush forests and dramatic Adirondack Mountains of northern New York and heads southwest past the Finger Lakes (where, tired of roughing it, you might want to make a sidetrip to one of the many surprisingly fine local wineries).

Then it's on to such treasures as the caves and gorges of Ohio's Hocking Hills State Park; the multicolored cliffs of Michigan's Pictured Rocks National Lakeshore (on Lake Superior); the source of the Mississippi in Minnesota; and some of the last remaining tallgrass prairie in North Dakota's Sheyenne National Grasslands.

CHAPTER TEN

© Kevin Schafer/Tom Stack & Associates

HIKING THE WORLD

Okay. You've hiked the entire length of the Appalachian Trail. You've back-packed across the Yukon tundra, trekked Alaskan mountain passes, camped on every beach between San Diego and Vancouver. Now you're ready for a new thrill.

Or perhaps you've only done a bit of car-camping in North America. Maybe the fiery foliage of the northeast bores you, the knife-sharp ridges of the North Cascades leave you cold, the western deserts just don't haunt your dreams. You want something different, something more exotic, something that goes one step beyond your average trip to the closest trail. You want a backpacking trip that will brand itself forever in your memory.

How about scaling Mt. Kilimanjaro? Visiting the hill tribes of Thailand? Bushwalking Australia's last rain forests? These are only three of the dozens of choices now available to the enterprising backpacker with a passport and a taste for the exotic.

There's never been a better time to take an international backpacking adventure. More and more tour operators have begun to cater to individuals whose idea of a good trip does not involve luxury hotels and air-conditioned buses. At last, these adventure-travel companies (some of which are listed on pages 170 - 171) seem to be realizing that there's a new generation of travelers who want to catch a glimpse (or more than a glimpse) of the world as it once was, not as it will be.

Every year, the opportunities are even more varied. Countries from Bhutan to Zimbabwe are creating new trails, building new campgrounds, and training local guides to deal with the thousands of people who want to catch a glimpse of a world outside the influence of television, of *USA Today*, of the golden arches.

Andean scene, Peru.

The list below is, of course, incomplete. (In Europe and elsewhere, for example, nearly anywhere with a trail and campsites is a suitable place to backpack.) But at least it should give a sense of the thrilling variety of trips awaiting you.

FIVE CLASSIC HIKES

PERU: THE INCA TRAIL TO MACHU PICCHU

To hike this famous thirty-five-mile trail leading from the banks of the Urubamba River to Machu Picchu, the renowned Lost City of the Incas, is to retrace the steps of ancient Inca royalty. The spectacular trail climbs to nearly fourteen thousand feet, wending its way past Inca tombs and terraced fields still tended by the descendants of the Incas, providing stunning views of nearby snow-capped peaks, as well as a wealth of fascinating plant and birdlife.

On the last day of the hike, trekkers pass through the stone Door of the Sun into Machu Picchu. Widely considered to be the most magnificent Indian ruins in South America, Machu Picchu is especially magical at dawn and dusk, when the fog rolls in from nearby jungle-clad mountains. Even the hardiest backpacker won't regret spending a night or two in the hotel on the grounds.

TANZANIA: CLIMBING MT. KILIMANJARO

The ascent of Kili, Africa's highest mountain, requires no pitons, no ice axes, no mountaineering experience. But it is a spectacularly beautiful—and at times quite demanding—trek, including nights in huts situated at nine thousand, twelve thousand, and fifteen thousand feet. You'll hike through bizarre mountain forests, over rubble-strewn slopes, and past the haunted, jagged peak of Kibo, the final resting place of the famous leopard in Hemingway's *The Snows of Kilimanjaro*. Finally you'll climb to the great Uhuru summit at 19,340 feet, where, surrounded by glaciers, you'll gaze down on all of Africa spread out below you.

Opposite page: Machu Picchu, Peru.

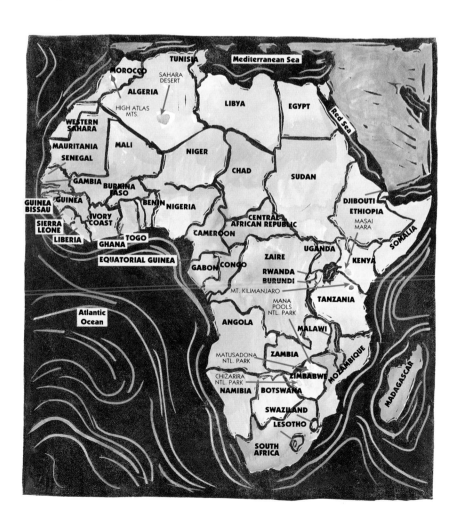

Opposite page: Hiking the Himalayas.

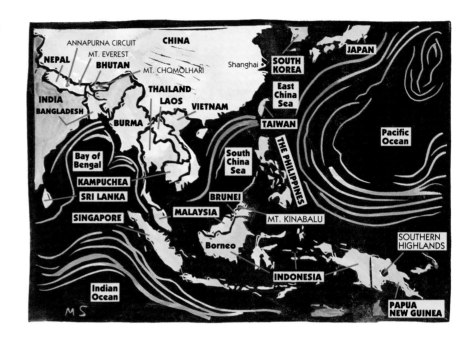

NEPAL: TREKKING EVEREST

Is there a more popular backpacking adventure than a trek around the base of Mt. Everest? This is the only place on earth where you can spend nights with Sherpa villagers, hike in the shadow of five of the eight highest mountains on earth, break camp on mornings so crystalline they will lighten your spirit. These delights and more await anyone who explores the spectacular land-scape stretching in all directions from the "Mother Goddess of the Snows"— as Everest is known in Tibetan.

Everest region, Nepal.

PAPUA NEW GUINEA: LIFE AMONG THE WIGMEN

The Southern Highlands of Papua New Guinea have an air of mystery, of ghostliness, found nowhere else. These dense, dark forests are home to gaudy butterflies, bizarre mammals, and the stunningly beautiful birds of paradise, creatures so unearthly they were once thought to be messengers from heaven.

The Southern Highlands are also home to the Huli Wigmen, a tribe (first contacted in the 1930s) whose men are renowned for their magnificent triangular headdresses, made of bird-of-paradise and parrot feathers, shells, beads, and the.wearer's own hair.

Several organizations now offer backpack trips through Huli territory. Groups hike past razor-sharp mountain ridges, wend their way through virtually untracked forests, and spend each night sleeping in Huli villages. If you're very lucky, your visit will coincide with a *sing-sing*—a village (or regional) meeting, performance, and feast that can last for days.

Huli Wigman, Papua New Guinea highlands.

© Larry Tackett/Tom Stack & Associates

NEW ZEALAND: WALKING THE MILFORD TRACK

At thirty-three miles, a hike of the entire Milford Track may not satisfy those seeking strenuous treks filled with breathtaking adventures. But this extremely popular route will please anyone looking for spectacular views.

Trips begin at Lake Te Anau in southern New Zealand and wind alongside rushing rivers, through the depths of glacial canyons up to windswept mountain passes, and past meadows alight with lilies and other flowers. Almost every step reveals another marvelous view: distant rivers far below, vast canyons cut into the earth, glittering lakes, and Milford Sound, New Zealand's most dramatic fjord and the hike's ultimate destination.

TREKKING THE MOUNTAIN KINGDOMS

ARGENTINA: ACONCAGUA, SOUTH AMERICA'S SUMMIT

At nearly 23,000 feet, Cerro Aconcagua is the highest mountain in the Western Hemisphere. Although the high peaks admit only the experienced mountaineer, both experienced hikers and fit beginners can enjoy trekking the lower slopes of the Aconcagua.

The highlight is certainly the hike to the base of the mountain's south face. Here, at 13,500 feet, trekkers can stand at the base of a sheer, nearly vertical wall of rock that rises almost two miles, nearly straight up.

BHUTAN: LAND OF THE DRAGON

Everest too popular for you? Annapurna too familiar? Maybe it's time to backpack the Dragon Kingdom: Bhutan, a land of spectacular scenery rarely

visited even by globe-trotting trekkers. Groups lead demanding hikes to the base of Mt. Chomolhari (sacred home of the Goddess of Longevity); the route leads past ruined temple-fortresses, cool evergreen forests filled with birds, meadows dotted with local yak-herders, and the breathtaking mountain scenery for which central Asia is justly famous.

CHILE: THE TOWERS OF PAINE

No place on earth can outdo the mystery and grandeur of Patagonia, the cold, windswept southern tip of South America. And no place in Patagonia is as spectacular as Paine National Park, home to the famous Towers of Paine. These granite peaks rise like enormous obelisks, towering six thousand feet and more above the region's frigid lakes, endless grasslands, and perilous abysses.

Visitors to the landscape that surrounds the Towers have the opportunity to explore the huge Grey Glacier, search for parrots, flamingos, and other unfamiliar birds on lakeshores and in ancient beech forests, and wonder at the power of a glacier that could carve such awe-inspiring mountains.

Paine National Park, Chile.

ECUADOR: COTOPAXI, THE PERFECT VOLCANO

Just thirty miles south of Quito—Ecuador's Andean capital—lies 19,348-foot Cotopaxi, a stunningly symmetrical, snow-capped volcano. The country's second highest mountain, it is also the tallest active volcano on earth. Although it has rarely erupted during the past century, it frequently emits clouds of steam. On any trail, scan the skies for the magnificent Andean condor, one of the world's largest birds. Unlike its cousin, the California condor, this enormous bird is still thriving.

Backpacking possibilities are abundant on the slopes of Cotopaxi, in the surrounding national park, and on the lesser peaks that flank the great volcano. Many trekkers choose the week-long circuit around the base of Cotopaxi, with side trips to ascend nearby mountains.

Previous pages: The Towers of Paine, Patagonia, Chile. Opposite page: On Cotopaxi.

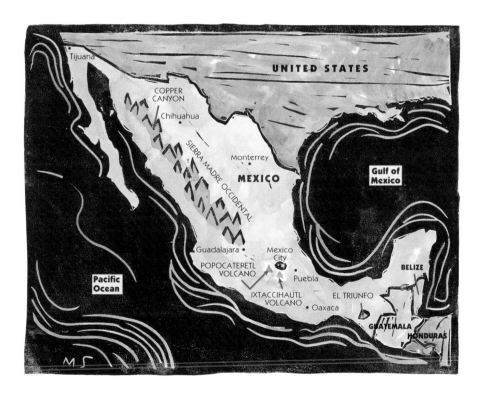

MEXICO: THE VOLCANOES

Not far from the great sprawl of Mexico City lies a pair of volcanoes that matches any in North America for its scenery and challenge. The hike up Popocatepetl, which reaches 17,887 feet, leads from the surrounding lowlands to the mountain's perfect cone.

Nearby lies Ixtaccihautl (17,343 feet), not a perfect cone, but a more difficult, and equally rewarding climb.

Opposite page: Annapurna Range, Nepal.

MOROCCO: THE HIGH ATLAS TREK

Morocco's High Atlas region is home to vast deserts, stark mountains, ancient forests, and the proud, independent Berbers. A trek in this region will take you through Berber villages that have existed unchanged for generations; over rocky passes two miles above sea level; and to the summit of little-known Mt. M'Goun, with its unparalleled views of the Sahara Desert.

NEPAL: THE ANNAPURNA CIRCUIT

Everyone's heard of Annapurna, at 26,540 feet, the world's tenth highest mountain. But only those who have trekked here know that there are several Annapurnas, enormous mountains—every one spectacular—that fringe the harsh Manang Valley for sixty-four miles. A hike amid the Annapurnas will take you past roaring rivers, forests of flowering rhododendrons, rice fields of the Gurung tribe, and some of the most breathtaking mountain scenery on earth.

NEW ZEALAND: THE ST. JAMES WALKWAY

Don't come here if you're expecting twenty-thousand-foot peaks. But if you're looking for a gorgeous trek on New Zealand's South Island, and you find the Milford Track too tame and overpopulated, the St. James Walkway, set in the little-visited Spenser Mountains, may be a perfect option.

The Walkway stretches for forty-two miles of meadows, beech forests, and river valleys. Here you'll have the chance to glimpse some of New Zealand's unique birdlife; spend nights sleeping beneath countless southern constellations; and brave swinging wire bridges over treacherous gorges.

South face, Annapurna.

PERU: CONQUERING THE CORDILLERA BLANCA

Imagine a remote, unspoiled region containing forty mountains over nineteen thousand feet. A tropical mountain range where hikers can stroll across fifteen thousand-foot-high passes in cotton slacks and light jackets. A place where every day brings hidden waterfalls, and glimpses of lush valleys far below.

Welcome to Peru's Cordillera Blanca, one of the richest mountain ranges west of the Himalaya. Trekkers here have endless choices of different routes, but many concentrate on Huascaran National Park, home to eleven peaks above twenty thousand feet, topped by Huascaran, Peru's tallest mountain.

SIKKIM: TREKKING IN A HIDDEN COUNTRY

Northeast of India, nestled between Nepal and Bhutan, lies the tiny kingdom of Sikkim. Much of this mountainous country remains off-limits to outsiders, but some of the most spectacular regions are now open to dedicated trekkers.

Sikkim's scenery is magnificent: blooming rhododendrons, orchids, and lilies, lush montane forests, green rice paddies, and extraordinary mountain views, including 28,168-foot Kangchengjunga, the world's third tallest peak.

SOVIET UNION: SCALING ELBRUS

Every Russian trekker knows about the Caucasus Mountains—but few outsiders are familiar with these rugged and beautiful peaks. Backpackers hike through the flower-filled alpine fields of the Baksan and Azhilisu valleys and climb the slopes of 18,841-foot Mt. Elbrus, the tallest mountain in Europe.

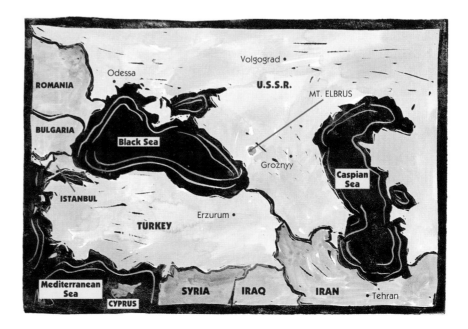

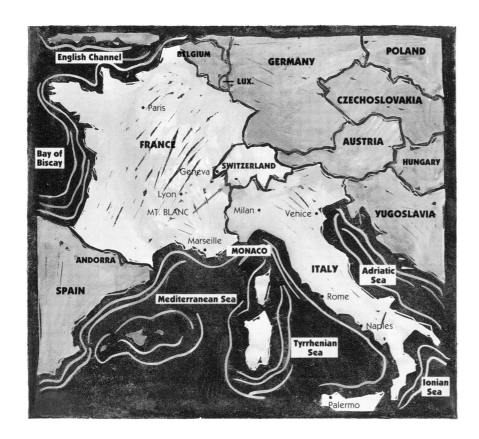

SWITZERLAND: MONT BLANC, A CLASSIC TREK

Want to hike through France and Italy, as well as Switzerland? Want to be dazzled by booming glaciers, jagged mountains, and flower-filled alpine meadows? Want to camp in the shadow of the Alps' highest peak?

Then follow in the footsteps of generations of hikers and take the classic Mont Blanc trek. Here is a Europe far removed from familiar orderly Swiss villages, cosmopolitan French cafés, and sunny Italian villas. It's a taste of a continent as it once was and never will be again . . . and it's not to be missed.

Near Zermatt, Switzerland.

EXPLORING THE LAST WILD FORESTS

AUSTRALIA: THE WONDERS OF LAMINGTON

Queensland, Australia's northeastern state, is also the location of the country's only rain forests. Although much has been cleared for building and agriculture, many areas have been protected as national parks. Perhaps the most beautiful is Lamington National Park (only sixty miles from big-city Brisbane), with its rolling forested hills, valleys swathed in vines, and 500 waterfalls. Lamington is an ideal place for a short "bushwalk"—or days of exploration.

While bushwalking the Toolona Creek circuit, the Coomera Circuit, or any other of dozens of trails, watch for king parrots, crimson rosellas, and many other gaudy parrots; platypuses swimming in clear pools; and padmelons, potoroos, and other odd marsupials in forest glades and meadows. You're bound to spot something memorable.

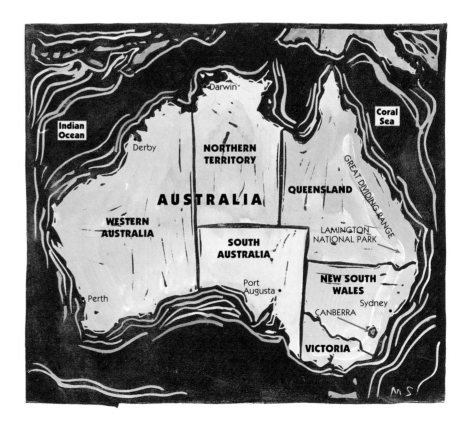

BORNEO: THE JUNGLES OF KINABALU

Borneo: Island home to orangutans (locally called the "Old Men of the Jungle"), Iban headhunters, giant hornbills and other fascinating birds, and some of the steamiest, densest, and most fascinating rain forest left in Asia.

Borneo is also the location of Mt. Kinabalu National Park, one of the few parks that provides easy access to the country's remaining forests. Hikers here are awakened by the thrilling dawn chorus of what seems like every bird on earth. A highlight will be the dayhike up Mt. Kinabalu (13,455 feet) itself, which leads from the lowland jungles up to the spectacularly rocky summit.

Orangutan at home in Borneo.

Mt. Kinabalu, Borneo.

Previous pages: Copper Canyon, Mexico.

MEXICO: FOREST IN THE CLOUDS

The trail that leads up beautiful El Triunfo in southeastern Mexico is an easy three-day hike—but it's also much more. It's an escape from the ravages that civilization has wrought on so much tropical forest, and a chance to explore one of the rarest, most magnificent, and least accessible environments on earth: the cloud forest.

El Triunfo's cloud forest is a magical, mystical place, filled with ten-foot-tall ferns and trees hung with moss, orchids, and epiphytes, plants that draw their nutrients from the air. This forest is also home to the bizarre and rare horned guan and the elusive resplendent quetzal, perhaps the most beautiful bird on earth. Stay awhile.

TAHITI: BEACHES, REEFS, AND JUNGLES

On the southeast edge of Tahiti, far from the resorts that line the island's incomparable beaches, lies a peninsula that still retains much of that magical aura that has entranced visitors for centuries. It's called Tahiti-Iti (Little Tahiti), and though well known by the French, it's just being discovered by North American hikers.

The trail skirts the coastline, taking hikers along spectacular beaches, across rocky streams, and past spectacular headlands. But perhaps the trail's greatest treat is the glimpse it gives of the rain forests that once covered Tahiti; with their buttressed trees, flowering hibiscus, and rare and glorious birdlife, the forests of Tahiti-Iti are among the most splendid left on earth.

© Ed Robinson/Tom Stack & Associates

The magical aura of the Lau Islands in Fiji has enticed visitors for centuries.

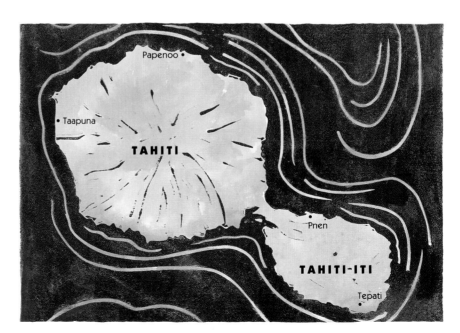

VENEZUELA: JOURNEY TO THE LOST WORLD

There's a region of extraordinary beauty and mystery in southeastern Venezuela where the bizarre tepuis, flat-topped mountains that rise like ancient monoliths out of the tangled jungle, lie. In Arthur Conan Doyle's classic *The Lost World*, a team of intrepid explorers found dinosaurs and other thought-to-be extinct creatures on a mountain inspired by nine-thousand-foot Mt. Roraima, the grandest tepui of all.

Dinosaurs may not actually survive on the tepuis, but hundreds of plants and animals found nowhere else on earth thrive on these isolated mountains. A six-day backpack that takes you up the slopes of Mt. Roraima requires hiking over steep, muddy, and slippery trails, but the bizarre dwarf forests, gemlike birds, and sense of discovery are more than worth it.

WILDLIFE WALKS

BRAZIL: ADVENTURING IN THE PANTANAL

There is one area of South America that can almost match Africa for the abundance, variety, and beauty of its wildlife. This is the Pantanal of Brazil, famous for its vast reedy swamps, its mammals, and its inaccessibility. Now, however, the Pantanal is becoming easier to reach, and intrepid explorers can finally delight in tapirs, capybaras, tropical cats, and other animals better seen here than anywhere else on the continent. While you're here, don't miss a side trip to the endangered Brazilian Amazon—not easy to backpack into, but worth a trip anyway.

GALAPAGOS: THE ENCHANTED ISLANDS

Most visitors to the Galapagos Islands (located about six hundred miles west of Ecuador) stay on yachts, taking only short day trips onto the islands themselves to view the sea lions, tortoises, albatrosses, and marine iguanas (as well as the finches that inspired Charles Darwin's *Origin of the Species*).

It is possible, however, to join a group that will take you off the beaten track to the islands' harsh interiors. Short but strenuous treks will take you over rugged lava flows, through desert landscapes filled with birds and animals, to the rim of spectacular volcanoes. The highlight may be Volcan Alcedo, home to gloppy mud pools that attract dozens of bizarre giant tortoises, rare elsewhere in the Galapagos.

Land iguana, Galapagos.

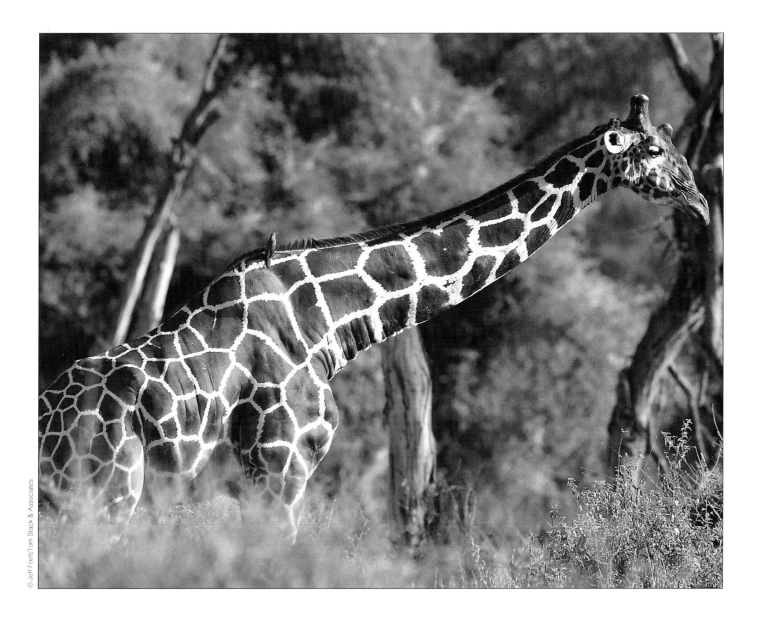

© Jeff Foott/Tom Stack & Associates

© Joe McDonald/Tom Stack & Associates

KENYA: STALKING BIG GAME

Anyone who's ever been to East Africa (or even planned a trip there) knows how hard it is to hike where the animals are. With good reason, the national parks tend to be off-limits to foot traffic. If you want to see wildebeest herds, lions lazing in the sun, or elephants taking a mud bath, you have to be prepared to do it from inside a minivan or Land-Rover.

There are exceptions, however. Several groups now offer Kenya walking safaris that skirt Masai Mara and other parks; explore Shaba Reserve (famous as the home of George and Joy Adamson and Elsa, the heroine of *Born Free*); and plunge deep into the heart of the Loita Hills. You may not see as much as you would from a car—but the experience of being eye to eye with a herd of zebra or an elephant is thrilling.

Opposite page: Masai Mara Game Reserve.
Above: Samburu Game Reserve.

An African elephant makes its home in the Masai Mara National Park, Kenya.

ZIMBABWE: LAST REFUGE OF THE GREAT ELEPHANTS

Though far less well known than Kenya and Tanzania's parks, the wilderness areas of Zimbabwe harbor some of the finest wildlife spectacles left on earth. Zimbabwe is also a country where hiking tours are still possible, where (accompanied by an expert tracker/guard) you can walk quietly—and a bit nervously—through a glade, never knowing if you'll suddenly come upon a lion, a leopard, a hyena—or just a comical warthog or flighty antelope resting inconspicuously around the bend.

Many groups choose to visit Mana Pools, Chizarira, and Matusadona National Parks, remarkably untouristy reserves where walking safaris are permitted. Elephant, lion, Cape buffalo, and rhino are all possible sightings, while antelope, abundant birds, and unmatched views are guaranteed.

DESERT TREKS

ALGERIA: INTO THE SAHARA

Though not a true hike (transportation is by camel), a journey across a section of the Sahara provides a thrilling opportunity to explore one of the most beautiful, unforgiving environments on earth.

Most of the Sahara Desert trips begin in villages inhabited by the Touaregs, desert dwellers for countless generations. Then it's on into the Sahara, with its spectacular domes, gorges, and endless sand dunes. A special treat: rock paintings, millennia old, that depict the animals of an earlier, less demanding desert.

MEXICO: COPPER, THE UNKNOWN CANYON

Actually a group of canyons covering more than ten thousand square miles, the Barranca de Cobre (Copper Canyon), hidden in the remote Sierra Madre Occidental in northwest Mexico, is one of the world's most spectacular—and least known—natural landmarks. Five times the size of the Grand Canyon, and far deeper, Copper Canyon's harsh near-desert landscape has been home to generations of cave-dwelling Tarahumara Indians. Today, trekkers can follow Indian trails along sheer cliffs; visit villages barely touched by modern civilization; and perhaps have the privilege of hiking where no previous trekker has ever trod.

CULTURE AND CULTURES

ENGLAND: LAKES AND LITERATURE

Rarely has a region been more beautifully described than England's Lake District was by William Wordsworth. The poet spent much of his life in the North Country, immortalizing it in his *Guide to the Lakes* and many poems. Today, hikers can trace routes described by Wordsworth, admiring the mix of mountains, streams, and lakes, while visiting charming villages and landmarks with charming names like Borowdale, St. Bees Head, and Easedale Tarn.

IRIAN JAYA: THE EDGE OF THE WORLD

Irian Jaya, which comprises the western half of the island of New Guinea, is even less well known and less traveled than its neighbor, Papua New Guinea. Yet it is home to beautiful birds and flowers, extraordinary jungle and mountain scenery—and some of the most fascinating, least acculturated tribal peoples on earth.

Rugged treks along centuries-old trading routes will bring you into contact with several different tribes, including the Dani, with their colorful feather headdresses; the Yali, who wear ornamental waist hoops; and the nearly naked (and virtually uncontacted) lowland Asmat people. A carefully planned, low-impact visit to Irian Jaya is one of the last chances to escape the ever-spreading sameness of the modern world.

KENYA: AMONG THE MASAI

Not every trip to Africa concentrates entirely on the continent's grand wildlife. Some choose instead to spend time with the famous pastoral Masai, whose lives revolve around their carefully tended cattle herds. Treks through the beautiful savanna country south of Nairobi bring groups in contact with several villages where the Masai maintain their traditional lifestyle.

MALI: A VISIT WITH THE DOGONS

Along the Niger River in the remote nation of Mali live the Dogon, a people who still live much as they have for centuries. Camping safaris now offer the opportunity to trek from village to village, skirting sheer cliffs pocked with ancient tombs, enjoying Dogon hospitality and marveling at their ornate huts topped with beautifully wrought conical roofs.

This village is home to the Dogon, a people of Mali who still live much as they have for centuries.

NEPAL: SHERPA LIFE

Anyone who has ever visited Nepal has seen the Sherpas, who function as porters on every Himalayan trek. But Sherpa life is far richer and more complex than that spied by most outsiders. By going off the beaten track (or joining a group that does), finding an interpreter to help you talk with the Sherpas, and visiting Buddhist monasteries and Namche Bazaar—the central Sherpa market—you can at least gain a taste of these peoples' deeply religious lives.

Crossing a canyon, Nepal.

Sherpas (left) function as porters on every Himalayan trek.

SPAIN: THE HILLS OF ANDALUSIA

Behind the beach resorts, the bustle of Madrid, and the architecture of Barcelona, there's another Spain. This Spain features spectacular mountains, lush farmlands, and villages that retain the charm of their Moorish and Spanish influences. Don't miss a stop at Trevelez, the country's highest village and one of its most beautiful.

THAILAND: A GLIMPSE OF THE HILL TRIBES

Most visitors to Thailand see only garish Bangkok, or perhaps the stunning city of Chiang Mai, with its ornate temples and magnificent scenery. But for those with a taste for adventure and a love of backpacking, Thailand can offer much more: a window onto an unspoiled traditional culture not yet turned into a tourist attraction.

The Karen, the Shan, the Lahu—these are just a few of the hill tribes of northern Thailand. Each has its own culture, its own traditions, its own relationship with the nearby jungles and mountains. Trek here and you'll get a taste of the great—and refreshing—cultural variety that still exists among the people of the earth.

Opposite page: The outback in bloom.
Right: Red kangaroo.

© John Cancalosi/Tom Stack & Associates

JUST ONE MORE: A NEW LONG TRAIL

AUSTRALIA: DOWN UNDER'S LONGEST TRAIL

Planning a trip Down Under? Have a few months to spend hiking? Then consider the new National Bicentennial Trail, a wonderful hike that wends for 3,140 miles along the eastern edge of the great island continent.

Unveiled in 1988 (Australia's bicentennial), the trail takes you through pristine rain forests inhabited by gaudy birds, enormous butterflies, and tree-climbing kangaroos; along the ancient mountains of the Great Dividing Range; through parrot-filled savannas; and even through the city of Canberra. If you finish the trail and still want more, various side trips carry you into even wilder (and frequently more challenging) terrain.

© Dave Watts/Tom Stack & Associates

E P I L O G U E

Anyone who has been in a mountain store recently will agree: Outdoor gear has come a long way from the age of heavyweight leather boots and drab canvas tents. These days, tents, packs, sleeping bags, and apparel all seem to be made of high-tech fabrics with space-age names in colors never seen in nature. And the changes keep coming. In fact, the rate of new developments in the outdoor gear market has accelerated to such a degree that it seems as if new fabrics and designs hit the stores every month.

What will the future bring? Gear manufacturers have always and will always contend with the same basic challenge—how to create long-lasting, lightweight, well-fitting high-performance gear. While all the pros agree they've come a long way, they also suggest that there are even more changes in store. Designers no longer just sit at drafting tables sketching their ideas— they work in laboratories developing new fabrics, experimenting with new

Paria Canyon, Utah.

© Spencer Swanger/Tom Stack & Associates

coatings, and combining them in unforeseen ways. As one company spokesperson said, "We are entering an age of better living through modern chemistry."

All seem to agree that while synthetics provide unmatched strength and lightness, they aren't as durable as many natural fabrics. When exposed to light, especially at high altitudes, today's synthetics degrade. Tomorrow's probably won't . . . at least not as quickly.

In the meantime, manufacturers seem to be committed to a compromise position: Taking the best that synthetics and natural fibers have to offer and combining them both in one garment or product. Thus, a high-performance hiking boot will likely be made of a series of synthetic materials to create a lightweight, comfortable, waterproof system that will be reinforced by leather at the points where extra strength is needed.

Manufacturers also seem committed to the idea that real aficionados will spend practically any amount of money to get top-of-the-line gear. Thus, as the state of the art becomes lighter and more complex, it will become increasingly less accessible to the average consumer. High-performance jackets costing $500 are in the future, and manufacturers are betting that they'll sell.

You won't have to buy high-priced products or nothing, however, as the market will also have plenty of room for moderately priced items that most of us can use. Now that outdoor apparel has developed a fashion sense, we are assured that there will always be well-made, great-looking, functional clothing. People will continue to buy it for hiking and climbing, but they'll be using it for gardening and golf as well.

So, it looks like it'll be easy enough to find well-functioning, hot-looking gear. That's the good news about the future.

Here's the bad news: As all but the most oblivious hiker must know by now, tomorrow's backpackers may find themselves all dressed up with no place to go.

The ongoing degradation of wilderness areas—both in North America and abroad—is proceeding at a terrifying pace. Many national parks have become overcrowded, with litter scattered over the backcountry, car exhaust polluting the air, thieves raiding campsites. Elsewhere, huge swathes of virgin forests are being cleared out, leaving twisted, burned stumps as mute testament to destroyed glory. Every year, it gets harder to find the pristine, seemingly unvisited lakes, mountains, and forests we remember so well.

Eroded trails: the road to run.

© Thomas Kitchin/Tom Stack & Associates

The situation internationally is, if anything, far worse. In Africa, Asia, and South America, even national parks aren't safe from the logger's chainsaw and the settler's axe. Some trails (such as the most popular Everest routes) have become almost unbearably trash-ridden, an embarrassment to any backpacker who truly loves untouched wilderness.

"Why are you trying to depress us?" you ask. "What are we supposed to do about these problems anyway? We go hiking to get away from the responsibilities of life, not to invite new ones."

Unfortunately, the good old days, when "Take only pictures, leave only footprints" was a sufficient hiker's creed, are long gone. Hikers must all do more now, take more responsibility for the integrity of our wild areas—or we risk having none left to hike in.

There are so many easy ways to help. Join a local hiking club—even if you never attend any of their functions, the money you give them in your annual dues will go to help fund worthy projects.

Join a national or international environmental organization that reflects your own priorities. (See the appendix for some suggestions.)

Send a donation to a specialized trail maintenance organization or to your favorite park.

Join a volunteer park clean-up. These usually occur in the fall and spring.

Check with a local trail maintenance organization to find out what sort of work is needed. Attend a trail maintenance workshop. Even if you've never wielded a crowbar, you'll be able to help. Some organizations ask local members to "adopt" a trail, to hike it regularly and take care of general clean-up and maintenance. If you're going to be hiking it anyway, why not?

Watch where you walk. Don't tread on fragile vegetation, and if you see that standing water is turning a section of trail to mush, step over it. Don't wear heavy-soled boots on fragile terrain.

Always pack out more than you bring in. Bring a plastic bag for garbage you find along the way.

Commit the rules of minimum-impact camping to memory, and abide by them always.

And, most importantly, educate yourself and your friends and family. Share with them the splendors of the wilderness and the pleasures of the trail. The more of us there are out there backpacking, the more influence we have, and the more likely it is that we'll have a wilderness to backpack in tomorrow.

Following pages: Wind River Mountains, Wyoming.

Every backpacker understands the importance of these words: If you pack it in, you *must* pack it out!

LET NO ONE SAY AND SAY IT TO YOUR SHAME THAT ALL WAS BEAUTY HERE UNTIL YOU CAME

A P P E N D I X

B ASIC C HECKLIST

Needless to say, no one list can possibly tell you what to pack for every backpacking trip you'll ever take. It all depends on the weather, the climate, how far you're going, how long you're going to be out, and your level of experience. So the following list is offered as a guideline, which must be adapted as you see fit.

C LOTHING

Rain suit

Boots

Socks

Camp shoes

Long underwear

Long pants

Shorts

Shirts

Sweater

Warm jacket

Shell

Gloves

Hat

Scarf

Bandanna

Bathing suit

S HELTER AND P ACKS

Tent with fly (or tarp or bivvy sack)

Groundsheet

Sleeping bag

Foam pad

Backpack

Daypack or fannypack

Extra tent stakes

Extra plastic bags

F OOD AND C OOKING

Stove

Fuel

Primer (if needed)

Plenty of food

Water bottles/canteens

Pots and cooking utensils

Cup

Spoon

Knife

Matches

Candle

Water purifier

N AVIGATION

Maps

Compass

Pencil

Paper/notebook

Whistle

T OOLS AND E XTRAS

Space blanket

First-aid kit

Sewing kit

Tent and waterproof repair kit

Binoculars

Camera

Film

Field guide

Safety pins

Flashlight

Lantern

Extra batteries

Book

Pedometer

Sunglasses

Extra glasses

Biodegradable soap/detergent

Towel

Toothbrush/toothpaste

Toilet paper

Latrine shovel

Fishing gear

Necessary permits

Plastic bags

O RGANIZATIONS

The following organizations work to preserve wilderness areas and/or maintain trails. Many offer hikes and walks through their local chapters. Contact them for information on programs in your area.

American Hiking Society

1015 31st St., NW

Washington, DC 20007

American Wilderness Alliance

4260 E. Evans Ave.

Denver, CO 80222

Appalachian Mountain Club
5 Joy St.
Boston, MA 02108

Appalachian Trail Conference
P.O. Box 807
Harpers Ferry, WV 25425

Canadian Hostelling Association
333 River Road
Tower A, 3rd Floor
Vanier City (Ottawa), ON K1L 8H9
Canada

Federation of Western Outdoor Clubs
5529 27th Ave., NE
Seattle, WA 98105

Keystone Trails Association
P.O. Box 251
Cogan Station, PA 17728

National Audubon Society
950 3rd Ave.
New York, NY 10022

Nature Conservancy
1815 North Lynn St.
Arlington, VA 22209

New England Trail Conference
33 Knollwood Dr.
East Longmeadow, MA 01028

New York–New Jersey Trail
   Conference
20 West 40th St.
P.O. Box 2250
New York, NY 10001

Sierra Club
530 Bush St.
San Francisco, CA 94108

Student Conservation Association
P.O. Box 550
Charleston, NH 03603

The Wilderness Society
900 17th St., NW
Washington, DC 20006

The Sierra Club, REI, and the Audubon Society offer national and international expeditions, as do the following outfitters (among others). Check the back of *Backpacker* or *Outside* magazine for a detailed listing.

Ecosummer Expeditions
1516 Duranleau St.
Vancouver, BC V6H 3S4
Canada

Mountain Travel
6420 Fairmount Ave.
El Cerrito, CA 94530

Overseas Adventure Travel
349 Broadway
Cambridge, MA 02139

Sobek
Box 1089
Angels Camp, CA 95222

Wilderness Travel
801 Allston Way
Berkeley, CA 94710

FOR FURTHER READING

BOOKS

Fletcher, Colin. *The Complete Walker III*. New York: Alfred A. Knopf, 1989.

Fodor's Worldwide Adventure Guide. New York: David McKay Company, 1979.

Government of British Columbia. *Outdoor Safety and Survival: A Pocket Companion*. Vancouver, British Columbia: Douglas & McIntyre, Publishers, 1984.

Jacobson, Cliff. *Camping Secrets: A Lexicon of Camping Tips Only the Experts Know*. Merrillville, Indiana: ICS Books, Inc., 1987.

Kals, W. S. *Land Navigation Book: The Sierra Club Guide to Map and Compass.* San Francisco: Sierra Club Books, 1983.

Kjellstrom, Bjorn. *Be Expert With Map and Compass.* New York: Charles Scribner's Sons, 1976.

Riviere, Bill. *The L.L. Bean Guide to the Outdoors.* New York: Random House, 1981.

Simer, Peter, and Sullivan, John. *The National Outdoor Leadership School's Wilderness Guide.* New York: Simon and Schuster, 1983.

Simmons, James. *The Big Book of Adventure Travel.* New York: Plume, 1990.

Thomas, Lynn. *The Backpacking Woman.* New York: Anchor Press/Doubleday, 1980.

PERIODICALS

Backpacker
33 E. Minor St.
Emmaus, PA 18098

Outdoor Woman
P.O. Box 834
Nyack, NY 10960

Outside
1165 N. Clark St.
Chicago, IL 60610

Walking News
P.O. Box 352
Canal St. Station
New York, NY 10013

MAIL-ORDER GEAR

If you know what you want, ordering your gear through the mail can be surprisingly convenient and inexpensive. There are many specialized manufacturers who will accept mail orders. Some of the more general retailers are listed below.

Patagonia
249 rue Paccard
74400 Chamonix
France

Campmor
810 Route 17 North
P.O. Box 999
Paramus, NJ 07652

Eastern Mountain Sports
Vose Farm Road
P.O. Box 811
Peterborough, NH 03458

Eddie Bauer
Fifth and Union
P.O. Box 3700
Seattle, WA 98130

L.L. Bean, Inc.
Freeport, ME 04033

Patagonia
Leopoldstrasse 47
8000 Munich 40
Germany

GEAR REPAIR

If your pack is ripped or your tent needs patching, you can try to fix it yourself, you can contact your local outdoor store for help—or you can get in touch with an expert.

Down East Service Center
75 Spring St.
New York, NY 10012

Patagonia Agency UK
Riverbank House, Putney Bridge
    Approach
London SW68JD
England

Patagonia of Canada
21 Water St., Ste. 400
Vancouver B.C.
V6B1A1 Canada

INDEX

METRIC CONVERSION CHART

Length

inches	x	2.5	=	centimeters
feet	x	30	=	centimeters
yards	x	0.9	=	meters
miles	x	1.6	=	kilometers

Mass (weight)

ounces	x	28	=	grams
pounds	x	0.45	=	kilograms

Temperature

To convert Fahrenheit degrees into
Centigrade, subtract 32, multiply by 5,
and divide by 9. To convert
Centigrade into Fahrenheit, multiply
by 9, divide by 5, add 32.